Civil War
Love Stories

Civil War
War
Love Stories

Haunting true tales told from both sides of the front lines

GILL PAUL

Introduction by
Bryan Guerrisi

METRO BOOKS
NEW YORK

For my father, John P. Paul

METRO BOOKS
New York

An Imprint of Sterling Publishing
387 Park Avenue South
New York, NY 10016

This book was conceived, designed, and produced by Ivy Press

Ivy Press

210 High Street, Lewes, East Sussex, BN7 2NS, UK

Creative Director Peter Bridgewater

Publisher Susan Kelly

Art Director Wayne Blades

Senior Editor Jayne Ansell

Designer Andrew Milne

Picture Researcher Shelley Noronha

ISBN 978-1-4351-4510-8

For information about custom editions, special sales, and premium and
corporate purchases, please contact Sterling Special Sales at 800-805-5489
or specialsales@sterlingpublishing.com.

Manufactured in China

Color origination by Ivy Press Reprographics

2 4 6 8 10 9 7 5 3 1

www.sterlingpublishing.com

CONTENTS

Introduction – 6

MAP
howing the
PARITIVE AREA
of the
RTHERN
AND
ERN STATES,
THE ROCKY MOUNTAINS.
1861.
LAKE SUPERIOR
LAKE MICHIGAN
I O W A
M I S S O U R I
RIVER
JEFFERSON CITY
ST LOUIS
K A N
INDIAN
TERRITORY
FORT GIBSON
RIVER
ARKANSAS
LITTLE ROCK
NASHVILLE
RED RIVER
T E X A S
AUSTIN
MISSISSIPPI
LOUISIANA
BATON ROUGE
G U L F
M E X I

Introduction

by Bryan Guerrisi

BATTLE OF CHANCELLORSVILLE.

The United States was less than 100 years old when the Civil War erupted. In only four years up to April 1865, the conflict would see more than 10,400 military engagements, from minor skirmishes in the New Mexico Territory and Texas to the mass-killing fields of Gettysburg and Petersburg.

The war exacted a grim toll on human life. More than 600,000 soldiers perished from the North and South combined, and there were approximately 75,000 additional civilian deaths; this amounted to some 3 percent of the total population of America. It remains the deadliest war in American history.

But what caused this nation in its infancy to enter into such a bloody conflict? As with most conflicts, the answer is somewhat complex; however, put simply, the American Civil War was the result of a culture clash between the industrialized North and the agrarian South. The North had a rapidly growing economy, based on family farms, industry, mining, commerce, and transportation. In contrast, the South's economy relied heavily on produce from plantations, the profitability of which was dependent upon the use of slaves doing hard manual labor, seven days a week. In 1860, the total gross domestic product of the United States totaled $1.9 billion, of which 92.5 percent came from the North. The South had few large cities and little manufacturing except in those areas bordered by Northern states.

OPPOSITE
Husbands and wives, parents, and their children were often separated after being bought by different owners at slave auctions.

BELOW
In November 1860, Lincoln was elected 16th President of the United States after winning over 40 percent of the votes. He made no secret of his anti-slavery views.

ABRAHAM LINCOLN'S RETURN HOME

Political disunion

From 1845 to 1854, the great potato famine drove nearly 2 million Irish people to come to the United States. This influx of immigrants from Ireland to Northern port cities such as New York and Boston meant more voters, with concomitant effects on the political map of the growing country. With the Northern population booming,

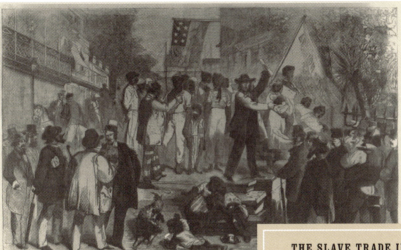

Northern politicians were gaining more power just as Southerners saw their power and influence in the federal government slowing slipping away.

In the election of 1860, the industrialized North had considerably more votes than the South, enabling Abraham Lincoln to win without even having been on the ballot sheet in ten Southern states. Lincoln had made no secret of his anti-slavery views during the election, and with him securing the presidency Southern leaders were increasingly concerned at what they felt was a lack of federal political concern for the pro-slavery South. They feared that Lincoln would not only end the expansion of slavery but send it on a course to extinction, and thus end their means of profitability.

Slowly but surely, the Southern slave states had become a minority in the House of Representatives, and were now faced with being a minority in the Senate and the Electoral College compared with the increasingly powerful North. Change to correct this imbalance, as the Southern states saw it, was urgently required.

THE SLAVE TRADE IN THE AMERICAN SOUTH

About 590,000 slaves came to North America between 1620 and 1865. Trading slaves was big business in the South; in one auction in 1859, 429 men, women, and children were sold to slave owners, fetching $303,850 (or $6.7 million in today's money). The format of an auction was often the same: slaves were displayed sometimes days in advance of sale, giving prospective buyers time to inspect them. They were then subjected to an examination, as slave owners tested their health and abilities. All this was carried out without protest from the slaves, who apparently sometimes displayed a joyful optimism if they liked the appearance of the proposed buyer, who might be a kind master.

RIGHT
The first shots of the Civil War were fired when Confederate general Beauregard attacked Fort Sumter in Charleston Harbor on April 12, 1861.

Secession from Lincoln's government

On December 20, 1860, the state of South Carolina seceded from the federal government. By February 1861, Mississippi, Florida, Alabama, Georgia, Louisiana, and Texas had followed South Carolina's lead. Together they formed the Confederate States of America, electing Jefferson Davis of Mississippi as president, and declaring Montgomery, Alabama the capital.

Anger erupted in the North at what they felt was a clear rebellion against the Union, and plans to put down the rebellion were quickly formed. In response, the Southern government began seizing arms and equipment in order to defend itself. Port cities such as New Orleans and Charleston needed to be secured so that commerce could flow easily in and out of the ports. Fort Sumter, situated in the middle of Charleston Harbor and held by Union forces, was a target of huge strategic importance for the South. Manned by a federal force of just 85 men, on April 12, 1861, the fort was quickly surrounded by South Carolina Militia units. The bombardment began, and just two days later the fort had surrendered.

Soon after the surrender President Lincoln called for a volunteer army to put a stop to the rebellion. Within two months, four more states had left the Union, while three other states had secessionist movements. Once Virginia had joined the Confederacy, the capital was moved from Montgomery to Richmond, Virginia to encourage the border states of Maryland, Kentucky, and Missouri to follow suit. But, on the newly elected president's orders, the imposition of martial law in Maryland and the arrest without trial of all prominent secessionists prevented Maryland from seceding and thus kept Washington, D.C. from being surrounded by Confederate territories. Thus, with Missouri voting to remain in the Union, and Kentucky declaring itself neutral, the stage was set for the War of Northern Aggression, as it was called in the South; or the Rebellion, as it was known in the North.

In the beginning both sides had more recruits than they could possibly train and equip. There remained a Victorian romanticism about the war; everyone felt it would be over quickly and would be relatively bloodless. Militia companies and regiments from across the country came together under names such as the Liberty Guards, the Session Guards, the Washington County Cold Steel Guards, the Garibaldi Guard, the Bucktails, and the Fire Zouaves. These companies and regiments from small towns and communities across the nation banded together to form the backbone of both the Northern and Southern armies. Training camps began springing up all over the country as both sides geared up to fight. One such camp in Harrisburg, Pennsylvania, known as Camp Curtin, would train over 300,000 Northern men for war.

Thousands of men volunteered to fight to preserve the Union in the North, and the same numbers acted to defend their rights in the South. In Pennsylvania the governor had to turn away whole regiments, after the state quota set by Lincoln for volunteers was filled. Large numbers of European immigrants joined the Union Army, often for the money and the staple diet on offer, many having arrived in America with nothing more than the clothes on their backs. It is estimated that 177,000 German immigrants and 144,000 Irish immigrants enlisted in the Union Army between 1861 and 1865.

BELOW
Three Confederate soldiers pose for a studio photograph in their new grey uniforms (below), while (bottom) six Union officers dressed in blue pose outside a tent at Camp Barry, near Washington, D.C. In the heat of battle, it could be hard to tell the uniforms apart.

The onset of war

At the onset of hostilities, the United States Army was 16,000-strong, with the bulk of it in far-off outposts in the western territories. After the fall of Fort Sumter, President Lincoln knew that he needed more manpower than his army could provide—and quickly. So a call was made for 75,000 volunteers to defend the Union. These men fought their first bloody battle on July 21, 1861, at what is known as the First Battle of Manassas or First Bull Run.

Almost a year later, the war still raged. In April 1862, Union general Ulysses S. Grant took his army up the Tennessee River, stopping at a place called Pittsburg Landing to await reinforcements. Confederate general Albert Sydney Johnston wanted to attack Grant before those reinforcements could reach him, so, on April 6, the Confederates launched a surprise attack on Grant's unsuspecting forces. But the attack stalled after Johnston was wounded during the battle, and that evening Grant's reinforcements arrived, allowing the Union Army to regain the ground it had lost on the following day. The Battle of Shiloh, as it was called, saw casualties in excess of 23,000, making it the bloodiest battle in U.S. history up to that point.

BELOW
The first battle of the war was fought at Bull Run: both sides were horrified by the casualty figures, with 2,896 Union soldiers lost and 1,982 Confederates.

On to Richmond

After his defeat at the First Battle of Manassas, Union commander Irvin McDowell was replaced with Major General George B. McClellan. Known as "Little Mac," McClellan was a master at both organization and training men; however, he lacked the ability to utilize his army effectively in combat, and over-estimated the strength of the Confederate Army. In the spring of 1862, McClellan assembled the largest army in United States history to that point—over 100,000 men—and sent them to the Virginia Peninsula on the James River to capture Richmond, the Confederate capital. What became known as the Peninsula Campaign was launched on March 25, 1862, and concluded with the withdrawal of Union forces after the Battle of Malvern Hill on July 1, 1862. The campaign, which included a series of battles known as the Seven Days, would cost the Union Army over 20,000 casualties.

Fresh from his victory at Second Manassas in August 1862, General Robert E. Lee felt the time was right to take the war north. Lee hoped that the citizens of Maryland would welcome his army as saviors, and put pressure on Washington, D.C. Lee's first objective was to take Harper's Ferry, Virginia, a stronghold of 12,000 Union troops under the command of Colonel Dixon Miles, and also the location of a large federal arsenal. General Thomas "Stonewall" Jackson's 30,000 men, under orders from Lee to capture the town, took up positions on the heights surrounding the settlement, and in three days had forced the surrender of over 12,000 men. With Harper's Ferry now in Confederate hands, Lee decided to continue with his invasion plans. On September 17, on the banks of Antietam Creek in the sleepy village of Sharpsburg, Maryland, more than 23,000 soldiers died in what is still the bloodiest

ABOVE
Pictures of fallen soldiers appalled the public, who had anticipated a relatively bloodless war.

WINCHESTER, VIRGINIA

Winchester, Virginia was perhaps the most strategic town in the entire country. Sitting at the northern end of the lower Shenandoah Valley, with four railroads and five major roads running through or near the town, it was a major transportation hub, connecting the western United States with Washington, D.C. In the course of the war, six forts and seven fortified batteries were built to protect this vitally important town. Between May 1861 and October 1864, thirteen battles or skirmishes occurred in and around Winchester, not including cavalry raids and reconnaissance by various forces. It is estimated that the town changed hands seventy-two times in four years of war.

" MAKE WAY FOR LIBERTY!"

ABOVE
*When African-
Americans began to
enlist, the Confederate
government declared
that, if captured,
they would be treated
as runaway slaves
and either killed or
returned to slavery.*

single day in American history. But the Battle of Antietam was also a stalemate. Lee survived to fight another day, while McClellan halted his invasion of the North.

Lincoln seized on the absence of defeat, casting it as a Unionist victory and announcing his Emancipation Proclamation; this declared all slaves in the Southern states free, and allowed African-Americans to enlist and fight. From this point on, the focus of the war in the North was not only on preserving the Union but also, as the South had feared all along, on abolishing slavery.

In the fall of 1862, Lincoln replaced McClellan for his failure to destroy Lee's army after the bloody battle at Antietam. By the end of that year, the Confederates had successfully defended their borders and Union forces were in disarray.

1863 . . . The tide turns

The following year, 1863, would prove pivotal for both armies. Following his poor performance at Fredericksburg, Lincoln replaced McClellan's replacement, Major General Ambrose Burnside, with Major General Joe Hooker. "Fighting" Joe Hooker, who had a reputation for not shying away from battle, began his campaign in April 1863 with the goal of outflanking Robert E. Lee's army and capturing Richmond.

The two armies met in the small hamlet of Chancellorsville, Virginia, with Lee gambling by dividing his numerically inferior force, sending Stonewall Jackson's men on a risky march around the Union Army's flank. At 5:30 p.m. on May 2, Jackson's 21,000 men came running out of the woods toward the Union Army's right flank, advancing 1¼ miles, and almost cutting the Union Army in two. The battle continued until May 6, when, after consulting with his generals, Hooker decided to pull Union forces back across the Rappahannock River. It was costly for both sides: Union casualties exceeded 17,000, while the Confederacy lost one of its most able commanders, Stonewall Jackson, who was shot in error by his own troops, in addition to over 13,000 men killed, wounded, or captured.

Following his victory, Lee decided again to take the war north, to give the state a break from the battles that had ravaged the landscape for almost two years. On June 3, Lee's army slipped away from the Union Army and began its march north to pursue what became the Gettysburg Campaign.

Hooker set off after Lee on June 14, only to resign his post later that month after a number of arguments with President Lincoln and his military advisors over battle plans. George Meade took over as commander of the Army of the Potomac, and in four days found himself engaged in the greatest battle of the war.

More than 164,000 men would fight on the rolling hills of the small Pennsylvania town of Gettysburg. For three days, July 1–3, Lee's army hurled itself at Meade's forces, trying to break the Union line that had bent and crumbled so many times in the past. But this time Meade's lines held firm. On the final day of the battle, Lee gambled again, sending 12,500 men on a frontal assault, known as Pickett's Charge, aimed at the center of the Union lines, figuring that here was the weak link. This time the gamble did not pay off. When the smoke had cleared at the end of the battle, the two armies had suffered over 51,000 casualties— the largest number in any single battle in the Civil War.

To add to the Confederate defeat at Gettysburg, the siege of Vicksburg in Mississippi ended the following day with the surrender of the city to General Ulysses S. Grant. Vicksburg was the last Confederate stronghold on the river; its surrender meant the army was cut off from this vital waterway. This was a turning point: though the war would last another year and a half, never again would the South be as close to independence as it was in the summer of 1863.

BELOW
Pickett's Charge at Gettysburg on July 3, 1863: 12,500 Confederate soldiers ran straight into Union artillery fire.

LINCOLN'S GENERALS

Throughout the first two years of war, Lincoln struggled to find a general who could win him battles. Command of the army would change hands no fewer than five times during the course of the conflict.

Major General Irvin McDowell commanded the army from May 1861 to July 25, 1861, but was replaced by **Major General George B. McClellan** following defeat at First Bull Run. McClellan was in command from July 26, 1861 to November 9, 1862. But he failed to follow Lee's army into Virginia after the Battle of Antietam, so Lincoln replaced him with **Major General Ambrose Burnside**.

Burnside was in charge from November 9, 1862 to January 26, 1863, but was promptly replaced by **Major General Joseph Hooker** after defeat at the Battle of Fredericksburg. Hooker held command from January 26, 1863 to June 28 that year. Though successful in battle, he resigned after a series of disputes with Lincoln and his military advisor.

Major General George Meade commanded the army throughout the rest of the war. But from May 1864, **Lieutenant General Ulysses S. Grant**, given the title of General-In-Chief Of All Union Armies, provided operational direction to Meade, though Meade himself retained formal command.

ABOVE
Major General George Meade was nicknamed "Old Snapping Turtle" by his men.

LEFT
General Ulysses S. Grant was an experienced horseman who led his troops into battle on horseback.

Grant versus Lee

The following year saw more bloodshed as the Confederacy
tried to hang onto its position. In March 1864, Lincoln appointed
Ulysses S. Grant Commander-In-Chief Of All Union Armies in the
field. Grant moved his headquarters to the Army of the Potomac,
still under the command of General Meade. The 1864 Overland
Campaign—a series of battles fought from May 4 to June 24—
proved that Grant was unlike any other commander Lee had
faced. Retreat was not an option for Grant, who was also helped
by a virtually endless supply of manpower, particularly after
Lincoln's Emancipation Proclamation allowed African-American
fighters to join the Union cause.

BELOW
*General Lee was
impeccably turned out
in full dress uniform,
with a well-polished
antique sword, when
he surrendered to
General Grant at
Appomattox Court
House in Virginia on
April 9, 1865.*

In 1864, Grant tried to advance on Petersburg, Virginia. He felt
that by taking the city he could isolate Richmond, forcing Lee
to move away from defending the Confederate
capital. However, the Confederates held out
at Petersburg for nine long months of trench
warfare as Grant tried unsuccessfully to
assault the city, by the end of which Lee's army
was in disarray as desertion and disease spread
through the ranks. Finally, on April 2, 1865,
Grant's army broke through the Confederate
lines and the end was nigh.

SURRENDER OF GEN. LEE!

"The Year of Jubilee has come! Let all the People Rejoice!"

200 GUNS WILL BE FIRED

On the Campus Martius,

AT 3 O'CLOCK TO-DAY, APRIL 10,

To Celebrate the Victories of our Armies.

Every Man, Woman and Child is hereby ordered to be on hand prepared to
Sing and Rejoice. The crowd are expected to join in singing Patriotic Songs.

ALL PLACES OF BUSINESS MUST BE CLOSED AT 2 O'CLOCK.

Hurrah for Grant and his noble Army.

By Order of the People.

The surrender of Lee

On April 3, 1865, Richmond finally fell to
the Union Army. Lee had hoped to head
west and regroup with General Joseph E.
Johnston's army in North Carolina, but
Grant's cavalry quickly cut off all avenues
of retreat, forcing Lee to surrender at
Appomattox Court House on April 9.

This did not quite signify the end of the
war. Roughly 175,000 Confederate soldiers
remained scattered throughout the South.
But, upon hearing the news from Virginia,
General Johnston surrendered the last
sizeable Confederate force to Union general
William T. Sherman on April 26, 1865, and
other smaller commands soon followed.

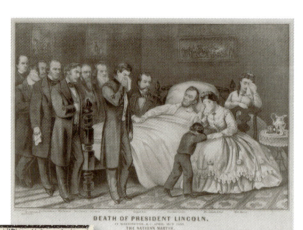

DEATH OF PRESIDENT LINCOLN.

OUR LOSS.

The Great National Calamity.

DEATH

OF THE

PRESIDENT.

Sad Details of the Terrible Event.

The Last Moments of the President.

SCENE AT THE DEATH BED.

The Life and Services of Mr. Lincoln.

IDENTIFICATION OF THE MURDERER.

John Wilkes Booth the Assassin.

ABOVE
*Just five days after
the South surrendered,
Lincoln became the first
American president to
be assassinated.*

A time for peace

With the end of hostilities, it was time for the nation to come together in peace; however, the night of April 14, 1865, brought anything but peace.

John Wilkes Booth, an actor of some fame and a Confederate sympathizer distraught over the recent surrender, learned that President Lincoln would be attending a play at Ford's Theatre in Washington, D.C., and decided to strike. At 10:20 p.m., Booth walked up to President Lincoln's balcony, pulled out a single-shot pistol, and at point-blank range shot the leader in the back of the head. The president died the next morning; Booth escaped the scene but was killed on April 26, 1865, while trying to evade capture.

Lincoln's plans for allowing the Southern states back into the Union were never fully known, but what transpired after the assassination of President Lincoln can be fairly described as a political civil war. Lincoln's vice president, Andrew Johnson, who now assumed the role of president, advanced a modest vision of reconciliation designed to bring the South back to normality as soon as possible. Johnson allowed the Southern states to elect civilian governors, and declared the war goals of national unity and an end to slavery achieved, and reconstruction thus completed. However, Congress was less than pleased with being so lenient toward the rebellious Southerners. The Northern congressmen refused to accept his terms, rejected their new Southern counter-parts, and by 1866 had broken with the president completely on the issue of reconstruction. A loose faction of the Republican Party, calling themselves Radical Republicans, gained congressional power that year. It was the aim of this militant group to impose stricter penalties against the South and ensure that Confederate nationalism was dead. President Johnson tried to resist, vetoing twenty-one bills passed by the radicals, only to have fifteen of them overridden and passed as law. One of them removed all civilian government in the former Confederacy, turning control of these former Confederate states over to the U.S. Army.

Thus the end of reconstruction was achieved in stages. By 1870, all former Confederate states had representation in Congress, though martial law still applied in the South. It was not until the economic panic of 1873 that the Radical Republicans' reign over Congress came to an end, with the Democratic Party making strong political gains in subsequent elections. Then, with the Compromise of 1877, military intervention in the South also ended, and with it reconstruction.

The American Civil War was unlike any other fought in America, as brother fought against brother, and neighbor against neighbor. Previously unknown towns and villages would be forever inscribed in the annals of history. And emerging from all this turmoil was a united nation that, having put an end to slavery, would become a beacon of freedom for the world.

ABOLITION

The Atlantic slave trade was abolished as early as 1807 in the United States, but internal slave trading went on until the 13th Amendment to the Constitution was added on December 6, 1865. This document would forever abolish the practice in the country. The text reads: "Neither slavery nor involuntary servitude, except as a punishment for crime whereof the party shall have been duly convicted, shall exist within the United States, or any place subject to their jurisdiction."

BELOW
Slavery was abolished in Missouri on January 11, 1865.

Thomas Jonathan Jackson
(January 21, 1824–May 10, 1863)

Mary Anna Morrison
(March 16, 1836–March 24, 1915)

MARRIED: *July 16, 1857*

ARMY: *Confederate*

RANK & DIVISION: *Major General in command of 2nd Corps*

BATTLES FOUGHT: *First Battle of Bull Run, Kernstown, McDowell, Front Royal, Winchester, Cross Keys, Port Republic, Seven Days Battles, Cedar Mountain, Second Battle of Bull Run, Harpers Ferry, Antietam, Fredericksburg, Chancellorsville*

MAP
OF THE
ACTION AT DRANES
December 20ᵗʰ 186
U.S.Forces Command
BRIG. GEN. E.O.C.C
Drawn by
H.H.Strickler, Co. A 9ᵗʰ Pa.
Published by authority o
HON.THE SECRETARY O
Office of the CHIEF OF ENGINEE
1875.

Thomas "Stonewall" & Mary Anna Jackson

During the early years of the war, Thomas Jackson—or "Stonewall" Jackson, as he came to be known—established his reputation as an ingenious military tactician and a key asset for the South. He was an odd man, often awkward in manner and eccentric in habits, but to his wife he was a tender, passionate, and devoted lover.

homas Jackson's early life was marked by one tragedy after another. His father and a sister died of typhoid when he was two; his mother died in childbirth when he was eight; and his older brother died of tuberculosis at the age of twenty, leaving Thomas with just one sibling, Laura Ann, and a half-brother. In his twenties he married Ellie Junkin, but the following year she died while giving birth to a stillborn child. So much bereavement heaped upon one so young could explain two aspects of Thomas's character: his fierce determination to succeed, and his unshakeable religious belief. As far as he was concerned, it was God who chose when people were struck down and it was not for us to question.

ABOVE
Ellie Junkin, Thomas's first wife, died just over a year after their marriage.

As a child, Thomas was raised by aunts and uncles and received little formal education; one of the family slaves helped him learn to read. Despite starting at such a disadvantage, he managed to struggle through the entrance exams for West Point military academy, working so hard that he excelled, overtaking most of his contemporaries. He served in the Mexican–American War, in the course of which he was promoted to the rank of major, then in 1851 he accepted a post teaching young recruits at the Virginia Military Institute in Lexington. He wasn't a universally popular teacher. The students called him Tom Fool and mocked his strict religious views behind his back, though no one dared do so to his face.

The love of a good woman

OPPOSITE
Thomas Jackson in his early twenties while serving in the Mexican–American War.

Mary Anna Morrison (known to all as Anna) met Thomas while she was in Lexington visiting her sister Isabella, who was married to a close friend of his. Her start in life had been in stark contrast

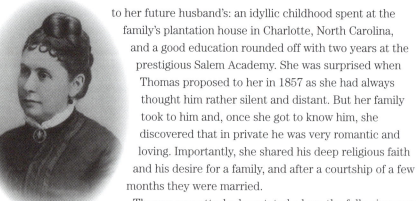

to her future husband's: an idyllic childhood spent at the family's plantation house in Charlotte, North Carolina, and a good education rounded off with two years at the prestigious Salem Academy. She was surprised when Thomas proposed to her in 1857 as she had always thought him rather silent and distant. But her family took to him and, once she got to know him, she discovered that in private he was very romantic and loving. Importantly, she shared his deep religious faith and his desire for a family, and after a courtship of a few months they were married.

Thomas was utterly devastated when, the following year, their first baby daughter died at only a few weeks old; it must have brought back all the earlier bereavements. But his young wife at least survived, and their shared grief seems to have drawn the couple closer together.

In 1859, they bought a townhouse in East Washington Street, Lexington, and began turning it into a comfortable home. They furnished it with pieces bought during trips to the North and created flower and vegetable gardens in which they both enjoyed working. They employed six slaves to help in the house and garden, and ran Sunday school classes in the town for both slaves and free blacks. According to Anna, Thomas "believed it was important and useful to put the strong hand of the Gospel under the ignorant African race, to lift them up."

The next two years were the happiest of Thomas's life, as he taught at the Virginia Military Institute by day and came home to his adoring wife each evening. The only cloud on the horizon was the lack of a child.

And then came war

Thomas Jackson did not support Secession, but in April 1851, when Abraham Lincoln called for every state to provide volunteers to suppress the "rebellion" in the South, he had no hesitation in deciding that his loyalties lay with the state of Virginia rather than the United States president. According to Anna, he "deplored the collision" and always felt that it could have been avoided, but when the chips were down he felt the best hope for the future of the South lay in a Christian Confederate government.

In June 1861, Jackson formed a brigade at Harpers Ferry from five regiments of Virginia infantry, and began drilling them relentlessly. At her husband's request, Anna found good homes for their slaves and closed their Lexington house before going to stay with friends. Presumably Thomas feared that living alone could put her in danger. Over the next two years, Thomas and Anna would spend most of their time apart. They wrote frequently, with letters full of affection and longing for each other. He called her "esposa" (wife) or "precious darling," and wrote describing the accommodation in which he was staying and the food he was being served, never failing to mention how much he thought of her and how he looked forward to seeing her "sunshiny face." She wrote back with wifely concern, urging him

SLAVERY IN THE AMERICAN SOUTH

In 1850, less than 25 percent of Southerners owned slaves, and half of these had fewer than five, who generally worked as house servants. However, the big coffee and tobacco plantation owners might have upwards of a hundred slaves working in the fields, with an astonishing one in seven of the entire population of America "owned" by someone else. While homeowners such as the Jacksons provided their slaves with Christian instruction and sufficient food and warmth, not everyone did likewise. The life expectancy of a slave was much lower than that of a free man, with only four in a hundred living to the age of sixty. Slave families could be split up and children sold at auction at their owner's whim; a slave owner could even kill one of his slaves without fear of legal sanction.

THE SALE.

to look after his health and make sure he got plenty of rest and good wholesome food. In August 1862, she even wrote to his physician, asking him to urge her husband to rest: "He is so self-sacrificing and is such a martyr to duty . . . I'm afraid he would sacrifice his life before he would give up."

> "He is so self-sacrificing and is such a martyr to duty . . . I'm afraid he would sacrifice his life before he would give up."

The first battle of the war, the Battle of Bull Run, took place on July 21 1861. The Unionists were so confident of victory that local people came out to sightsee—complete with picnic baskets and field glasses, as if it were a spectator sport—only to witness around 3,000 of their troops being either killed or injured. As the battle reached its climax, Jackson's brigade came to provide reinforcement on the strategic Henry Hill, and their staunch defense swung the day. It was reported that Brigadier General Bee rallied his troops, crying, "There is Jackson standing like a stone wall," and the nickname "Stonewall" attached itself to Thomas forever after.

Stonewall's brigade then headed into the Shenandoah Valley, where he triumphed in every battle he fought except Kernstown (and even that was only a tactical defeat). He proved to be a brilliant military tactician, helping the commander of the Confederate Army, General Robert E. Lee, to formulate strategy, and as a leader he was revered by his men. One of his soldiers wrote to a newspaper, "History contains no parallel case of devotion and affection equal to that of the Stonewall Brigade for Major General Jackson."

BELOW
Stonewall Jackson's brigade bore the brunt of the fighting at the Second Battle of Bull Run on August 29–30, 1862. It was a clear victory for the Confederates.

ABOVE *Jackson led his men into battle on horseback, accompanied by the regimental band playing martial songs.*

BELOW RIGHT *A Confederate songsheet, c.1861.*

REGIMENTAL BANDS

Military bands played an important role in maintaining the morale of the troops while they were on long marches, before going into battle, and even sometimes during the fighting. They mostly played brass and percussion instruments—trumpets, cornets, drums, and cymbals—but some had flutes as well. The music included lively marches or quicksteps, polkas and waltzes, emotional ballads, and even airs from the opera. According to his wife, Stonewall Jackson particularly enjoyed listening to band concerts but had virtually no talent for music himself. After she told him that "Dixie" was a popular song, he had her sing it over and over so he could memorize it. It became an unofficial anthem for the Confederates during the war.

THE GREAT TACTICIAN

Rather than confronting Union regiments of superior strength head-on, Stonewall Jackson opted for more devious strategies. He chose to "mystify, mislead, and surprise the enemy," throwing his men at the weakest point in the line, moving rapidly and appearing where his opponents least expected it. A case in point was his final battle at Chancellorsville, when he marched most of the Confederate army across the Union front and around for a devastating attack from the flank. He defended stubbornly at Antietam and Fredericksburg, with no regard for his own personal safety, believing that his life was in God's hands. Military historians still cite some of his Civil War maneuvers as among the finest examples of strategy ever seen, and there is no doubt that with his death the South lost one of its few advantages.

Stories circulated about his eccentricities, particularly with regard to his health: it was said he believed that if he ate pepper on his food, it caused an ache in his leg. He also thought one of his arms to be longer than the other, so he held it up frequently to equalize his circulation. He tried to observe the Sabbath, even during war, and would delay writing his letters to Anna until Mondays to avoid them being in transit on Sundays. He also tried to avoid fighting on Sundays, although this was not always achievable given events on the ground.

As a general he was strict, and insubordination was vigorously punished. But he commanded the respect of those he led because he was a winner—and by the winter of 1861–62, the Confederates badly needed winners.

A child is born

Thomas told his wife that he wouldn't write to her about military matters because it would be "unofficerlike," but often he couldn't resist boasting of his triumphs: "Whilst great credit is due to other parts of our gallant army, God made my brigade more instrumental than any other in repulsing the main attack," he wrote after First Bull Run.

Thomas and Anna were reunited for the winter of 1861–62 when they stayed with the Reverend James Graham's family in Winchester. Just before she left, in March 1862, the couple was overjoyed to learn that Anna was pregnant, but they could not have known that thirteen months would pass before they would see each other again. "My heart is just overflowing with love for my little darling wife," Thomas wrote soon after her departure, though he must

ABOVE
A print made in 1866, imagining the Jackson family as they might have been.

"My heart is just overflowing with love for my little darling wife."

have been desperately worried for the safety of his wife and their baby. On November 23, 1862, he received word of the birth of his daughter, at a healthy eight and a half pounds, and wrote back asking that she be named Julia Laura, after his mother and sister. "Give the baby-daughter a shower of kisses from her father," he asked, "and tell her that he loves her better than . . . all the other babies in the world." While overjoyed by the news, and desperate to see his child, still he fretted: "I am sometimes afraid that you will make such an idol of that baby that God will take her from us," he wrote in one letter to Anna—an understandable reaction, given his history of losing loved ones.

Laura was five months old before her father got to meet her, when mother and daughter spent nine days with him near Fredericksburg in April 1863. Laura greeted him with a bright smile and won his heart in an instant, although he still admonished his wife not to spoil her. On the Sabbath, Anna and Thomas went to a religious service held within a tent in the army camp, then spent the afternoon together. The next day, though, on April 29, he was forced to send her back to Richmond, as news came that the Union army was approaching and confrontation seemed imminent.

OPPOSITE
At Chancellorsville, on May 2, 1863, Jackson led a devastating surprise attack on the Union flank.

ABOVE
*Julia Laura Jackson
had no memories of her
famous father, the man
who, on his deathbed,
called her "darling little
sweet one."*

An accident leads to a tragedy

On May 1, Jackson's divisions hit back at the advancing Unionists in the Battle of Chancellorsville, startling them and forcing them to withdraw. During the evening of the 2nd, when he rode out to gather intelligence from his troops, some jumpy Confederate guards accidentally opened fire on their party and Thomas was wounded in the left shoulder, arm, and right hand. He was taken to a field hospital where the decision was made that his arm could not be saved, and the following morning it was amputated by chief surgeon Dr. Hunter McGuire. He was moved to a nearby plantation house to recuperate and Anna was sent for, but difficulties in communication and transport meant it took her five days to get there, and by that time her husband had succumbed to pneumonia.

Anna found quite a different man from the one she had left just over a week earlier. He was flushed with fever, sedated by morphia, and covered in contusions, with thick bandaging marking the place where his left arm had been. When roused, he pronounced himself happy to see her and told her how much he loved her. Over the next few days, as he drifted in and out of consciousness, Anna sat with him, reading Psalms and talking quietly. When she brought baby Julia into the room, his face lit up and he murmured, "darling little sweet one."

Thomas had told Anna once that he would prefer to have some time for preparation before entering God's kingdom, so on May 10, as his breathing became more subdued and the doctors told her there was no hope, she took the opportunity to explain to him that he was not going to recover and to ask if he had any dying wishes. At first he seemed surprised, but then accepted the news peacefully.

Dr. McGuire noted his last words. He woke and in a delirious state cried out, "Order A.P. Hill to prepare for action! Tell Major Hawks . . ." He didn't finish the sentence but a sweet smile spread over his face, and he said, "Let us cross over the river, and rest under the shade of the trees." Then he died.

According to his wife, grown men wept openly at the loss.

The Confederacy mourns

After learning of Stonewall Jackson's injuries, Robert E. Lee wrote, "he has lost his left arm, but I my right," and when he died, Lee told his cook, "I am bleeding at the heart." It was a bitter blow for the Confederacy and a crushing personal loss for Anna, widowed and with a six-month-old baby daughter who would grow up without knowing her illustrious father.

Thomas's body was buried in a cemetery named after him in Lexington, Virginia, while his amputated arm was buried separately, near the field hospital where it had been removed. After the funeral, Anna returned to her father's house for the remainder of the war to concentrate on looking after her child. She wore widows' weeds for the rest of her life and never remarried. "Time softens, if it does not heal, the bitterest sorrow," she wrote in 1895.

> *"Time softens, if it does not heal, the bitterest sorrow."*

Their child, Julia Laura Jackson, married in 1885 and had two children, but in 1889 she died of typhoid fever and Anna stepped in to raise her grandchildren. She also devoted her time to charitable works, and took part in many Confederate societies and reunions. "The grand lessons of submission and fortitude of my husband's life gave me the strength and courage to persevere to the end," she said in the preface to her husband's memoirs, published in 1895. When she died, in 1915, she was buried in the Lexington cemetery that bore her husband's name, near the man who had so patently adored her.

RIGHT
Stonewall Jackson's grave in Lexington, Kentucky. Visitors often left lemons there because he was reputed to have had a fondness for the fruit.

THE GRAVE OF STONEWALL JACKSON.
LEXINGTON VIRGINIA

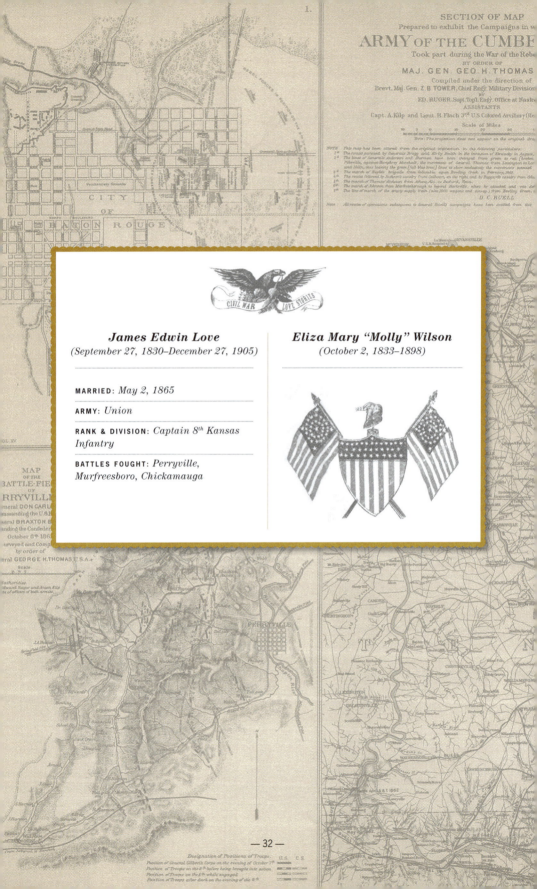

CIVIL WAR LOVE STORIES

James Edwin Love
(September 27, 1830–December 27, 1905)

Eliza Mary "Molly" Wilson
(October 2, 1833–1898)

MARRIED: *May 2, 1865*

ARMY: *Union*

RANK & DIVISION: *Captain 8th Kansas Infantry*

BATTLES FOUGHT: *Perryville, Murfreesboro, Chickamauga*

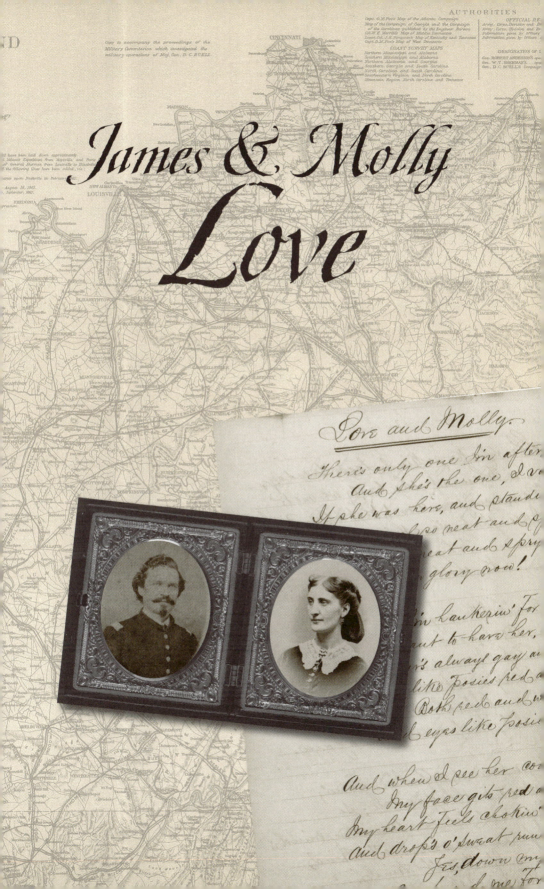

James & Molly
Love

**James and Molly met through his cousin Eliza, an occasion
James described from his point of view as "love at first sight."
By the time he headed off to war they had agreed to marry,
but had decided to keep the news a secret, which made it very
difficult for them to see each other over the next four years.**

Both James and Molly came from the north of Ireland: he from Bushmills, County Antrim, where the famous whisky was made, and she from Larne, where her father was a ship owner. James left school at thirteen and worked in various grocery stores and teahouses until, at the age of nineteen, he crossed the Atlantic with his brother Samuel to make his fortune in America. He went first to Cincinnati, where he lived with his Uncle Robert, then to St. Louis, where he stayed with his Aunt Mary Jane, and worked for a number of grocery stores in the city.

James was an ambitious boy, tempted by the fortunes he heard were to be made in the California Gold Rush. He almost headed out there in 1854 but was deterred by reports of the difficult conditions. Instead, he decided to seek gold in Australia and got a job on board a ship heading from New York to Melbourne, a voyage that took 103 days. He tried mining near the town of Ballarat, but after a year he'd failed to find much gold and returned to Melbourne, where he took a job as a shipping clerk. As he describes in his autobiography, "I had a list of Stores and Merchants who gave us a good commission on business taken to them." He obviously had an astute head for business and managed to amass some $6,000 over the next three years.

In 1858, he came back to St. Louis, where he bought four houses and a corner store, and became a prosperous businessman. It was then that his cousin Eliza introduced him to her husband's sister Molly, who had

BELOW
*In the early 1850s,
James worked in this
St. Louis grocery store
but said he found the
work "confining."*

emigrated to America with her mother and younger
sister after the death of her father in 1849. He did
not attempt to win her hand at first, because he
knew she would have many other offers and, he
wrote, "had a right to look above me." He was shy
and self-conscious around her, and even flirted
with her sister Sallie, all the while dissecting
Molly's "every thought & act."

Several times he tried to pluck up the courage
to propose to Molly, but his resolve would fail.
On one occasion he had determined to do it on a
particular day, only to hear that one of her brothers
had died, forcing him to postpone for several months.
But when he did finally venture to ask, Molly agreed
straightaway, only requesting that they not tell
her family just yet but leave it until after the war
was over, assuming as many did that it would end
quickly. Unable to believe his luck that she had
accepted, James agreed, unaware of quite how
long an engagement it would turn out to be.

"All my hopes of Heaven & earth depend on you,"

The language of flowers

With Molly's approval, James signed up to serve three months
with the 5th United States Reserve Corps, a home guard that he
hoped would keep him close at hand. She stayed in St. Louis with
her mother, her brothers John and Alexander, her sister Sallie,
and an aunt, and they began a long correspondence that would
see James write more than 170 letters to her throughout the
course of the war. They were chatty yet romantic, and well-
written, although he apologized for his poor writing style. "All my
hopes of Heaven & earth depend on you," he wrote to her, as his
company sailed down the Missouri River en route to Jefferson
City. He loved flowers, and sometimes sent pressed specimens in
his letters; for example, on May 19, 1862, he wrote, "After a ride
on the prairie and to the creek, I send you a sprig of the red,
white & blue I've got to beautify my table & perfume my tent."

Missouri was a key border state, with the third-largest corn
and pork production in the country, renowned for its horses and
mules, and its rich deposits of iron and lead. What is more, there
was an arsenal in St. Louis with 30,000 muskets, 90,000 pounds of

ABOVE
*James had a great
fondness for flowers
and often sent Molly
some pressed flowers
with his letters.*

— 35 —

Love and Molly.

There's only one I'm after,
   And she's the one, I vow!
If she was here, and standin' by,
She is a galso neat and spry,
      So neat and spry.
      I'd be in glory now!

It's so, — I'm hankerin' for her,
   And want to have her, too.
Her temper's always gay and bright,
Her face like posies red and white,
      Both red and white,
   And eyes like posies blue.

And when I see her comin',
   My face gits red at once;
My heart feels chokin'—like, and weak,
And drops o' sweat run down my cheek,
      Yes, down my cheek, —
   Confound me for a dunce!

ABOVE
James apologized for talking about his feelings "like a woman," but Molly must surely have been delighted by this poem, which describes her eyes as being "like posies blue."

RIGHT
Steamships flying the Union flag on the Tennessee River. The battles of Chattanooga, Knoxville, and Shiloh were all fought on its shores.

powder and forty cannons. After the state declared for the Union, its pro-Secession governor, Claiborne Fox Jackson, attempted to take control but was thwarted by General Nathaniel Lyon, who led the pro-Union Missouri Volunteers, including James's company, to secure the weaponry. Lyon went further, pursuing Jackson relentlessly and capturing his encampment near St. Louis. "Rather than concede . . . the right to dictate to my Government . . . I would see . . . every man, woman, and child in the State, dead and buried," Lyon warned.

Lyon's aggression pushed some who might otherwise have been Unionists towards the Confederate side, and small groups of guerrillas, or "bushwhackers," began to terrorize the region, making Missouri one of the most dangerous states for civilians throughout the war years.

James spent the three months of his first enlistment traveling up and down the Missouri River on steamships, securing supply lines without seeing any action. The Secessionists fled and, wherever they landed, Union sympathizers came out to greet them. But in Lexington, Kentucky, James's company was greeted by groups of ladies who waved

IMMIGRANT FIGHTERS

Almost a quarter of all Union soldiers had been born overseas, with the single biggest immigrant group being German (about 177,000), and the second biggest group Irish (144,000). The Irish generally had a reputation for being courageous in battle, but Germans were less highly thought of. They were nicknamed "Dutchmen" or "Hessians," and unfairly accused of attacking civilians. James Love writes that he played cards with "Swearing Dutch friends" on the steamship *A. McDowell,* and that they treated the ladies on board very badly, while the Americans and Irish extended them every courtesy. As the war progressed, immigrants sailed out from Europe and joined the Union Army straight off the boat in return for the bounty money on offer for signing up. Without their numbers, it would have been much harder for the North to win the war.

JAYHAWKERS AND BUSHWHACKERS

The word "jayhawker" was generally used to mean a guerrilla fighter sympathetic to the Union, particularly one from Kansas, while "bushwhackers" were sympathetic to the Confederates. The terms had been in use for a decade or more when war started and meanings became blurred, with "jayhawking" coming to mean theft in general. Bushwhackers tended to attack in ambushes (hence the name) and had a reputation for brutality, drawing few distinctions between combatant and non-combatant. William Quantrill was a notorious bushwhacker along the Missouri–Kansas border, responsible for the Lawrence Massacre in August 1863, when he led a band of men against the pro-Union town of Lawrence, Kansas, and had 183 men and boys as young as fourteen dragged from their beds and executed. Quantrill was killed in May 1865, but continued to inspire criminals such as Jesse and Frank James.

ABOVE *William Quantrill, bushwhacker*

the Confederate flag and sang "Dixie," the Confederate anthem, in an attempt to provoke a reaction. James and his comrades restrained themselves: "If they could only get us to insult or shoot a few ladies or children in a crowd, they think they could thus manufacture plenty of fresh Sympathy for the poor persecuted," he wrote to Molly. The rebels would not fight them directly, instead simply throwing away their arms and pretending to work innocently in the fields to evade capture.

In August 1861, James's period of service came to an end, and he traveled back to St. Louis for a couple of months, where he began to pursue a plan of putting together his own company of soldiers. As he said to Molly, he had "tried to act so that neither my own or my adopted country need ever be ashamed of me." He believed fervently in the Union cause, and went further than many in 1861 by wishing that the war might lead to the overthrow of slavery, writing, "may it not be a great gain to us & Mankind?"

James did manage to recruit a small company, which in February 1862 became attached to Company K of the 8th Kansas Infantry. They weren't involved in any major battles at that stage, but were tasked with patrolling the state border, and with returning horses and goods stolen by Confederate guerrilla fighters. As the months passed, he got bored with the daily routine in camp and wished he could invite Molly to join him—but how could he when they weren't married and no one even knew they were engaged? He asked her to consider breaking the news to her family, but she didn't think the time was right. "Oh that I could take unto myself wings like a dove & fly to you for I am a weary,

aweary positively for a sight of your
pleasant face," he wrote.

When he visited home briefly on May
31, 1862, he found Molly looking "thin,
weary and careworn," and begged her
to confide in him and stop being so
independent. James advised her that a
change of scene might help, or that she
should try to get out among her friends more, but she was
probably reluctant to travel far from home in St. Louis for fear
of bumping into guerrilla bands. They weren't able to spend
any time alone together, and while he "wished to talk of so
many things," he found himself frustratingly tongue-tied.

Why wouldn't she tell her family? Did she expect them to
disapprove? Was she reluctant to marry before the war was over
in case she found herself widowed? She seems to have cared
deeply for James, sending him a havelock cap to protect his fair
Irish skin from the sun, and a photograph of herself. "I shall never
be able to repay all the love you lavish on me," he wrote, and it
is clear from his letters that they had exchanged many kisses
in snatched moments of privacy. But still she wanted to keep
their engagement secret, and he had to respect her wishes.

"Oh that I could take unto myself wings like a dove & fly to you . . . "

ABOVE
*The Lawrence Massacre
on August 21, 1863, led
by William Quantrill:
he claimed he was
avenging wrongs done
by the Union Army
in Missouri.*

More than a quarter of all men who fought at the Battle of Chickamauga, which took place on September 19–20, 1863, were reported dead, wounded, or missing after the battle.

Battles and capture

In August 1862, James's unit was ordered to join Union general Rosecrans's forces in Tennessee to help drive the notorious Confederate general Braxton Bragg from the state. They marched through Mississippi, Alabama, and Tennessee, covering huge distances every day in pursuit of the rebel army. James complained frequently to Molly that their commander, Major General Buell, was too cowardly to confront Bragg and that the war could have been over much sooner: "I am tired of Buell ... He wants the war to last!! We do not!!!"

James saw his first major battle at Perryville, Kentucky, in October 1862. The Confederates won a tactical victory, but they were unable to hold the area and retreated back through Tennessee. James's company pursued them and spent the winter in Nashville. After the battle of Murfreesboro in December, he was involved in arresting stragglers and taking them prisoner, but through the spring of 1863 they stayed in camp, and the adventurous James grew ever more impatient. In late June, what is known as the Tullahoma Campaign began, and he was involved in frequent skirmishes with rebel troops, who ran away from head-on confrontation. On June 19, Rosecrans's army was camped on the banks of Chickamauga Creek when Braxton Bragg attacked, planning to encircle them and cut them off from their base at Chattanooga. The battle was fiercely fought over two days, and Rosecrans was forced to retreat, lucky to be able to escape with the remnants of his army. The Confederates had around 18,000 men killed or wounded and the Union Army about 16,000—among them James E. Love, who was hit in the leg.

As he lay unable to walk, with his leg broken and bleeding profusely, his own army retreated and James found himself watching from under a tree as Confederate soldiers rifled through the possessions of the dead. At last a young lieutenant of the Hospital Corps took him to a field hospital in a peach orchard, where he lay for ten days, only narrowly avoiding having his leg amputated because another wounded man from his own company bathed the wound regularly in cold spring water to prevent infection from setting in. After recovering sufficiently, James was shipped to Libby Prison in Richmond, where he stayed in the hospital wing until January 1864, able to walk only with the aid of crutches.

But the man who had traveled around the world as a youth wasn't going to be held back for long. There was a mass breakout from the prison in February 1864, when 109 Union soldiers escaped through tunnels; James wasn't fit enough to join in. He attempted to emulate them by digging a tunnel a few months later when he could walk more easily, but was detected by prison guards. He was transferred to Charleston and managed to escape from the train taking him there, but had to surrender after some farmers, "thinking it was runaway Negroes . . . ran us down with hounds and shot guns." In September he was sent to Columbia, South Carolina, where again he escaped. He was hoping to join General Sherman's army, which was marching through the state, but was again recaptured because "the guerrillas and pickets were so numerous between the two armies."

Next he was transferred to Charlotte, North Carolina, and managed his fourth escape by paying guards to help him. He and his comrades found a guide called Alec, a slave who was saving up to buy his freedom and who, in return for a fee, agreed to help them get across enemy lines.

From February to April 1865, James and his friends made their way home, over the Blue Ridge and Black Mountains, across rivers and valleys. "Our feet were terribly blistered, our whole bodies

sore and tired, but we made it in the rain," he wrote. It was an incredible journey, which he described in the autobiography he wrote for his children in later life.

After all the months of silence, Molly must surely have feared he was dead. When he knocked on her front door, limping and probably much aged by the elements, she fell into his arms, overcome with relief. They married in St. Louis on May 2, 1865, and made their home there, having four children—a son and three daughters. With his business skills, James became a successful grocery merchant, and was able to build a smart house for his family.

In April 1862, he had written to Molly that, in his absence, "there will be such a long bill of kisses due—I fear I never can collect them all." After almost four years of separation, it's lucky that they had thirty-three years of marriage in which to make up for lost time.

> *"there will be such a long bill of kisses due— I fear I never can collect them all."*

THE LIBBY PRISON BREAKOUT

During the winter of 1863–64, 1,200 Union prisoners were detained on the second and third floors of an old warehouse on the James River in Richmond, Virginia. From the moment they arrived, Colonel Thomas E. Rose and Major A. G. Hamilton were determined to escape, and they soon came up with a plan. In the basement, there was an old storeroom known as "Rat Hell," being overrun with hundreds of rats. They created a tunnel down to it through the chimney of a stove on the first floor, then started digging out through the floor of Rat Hell. It took them seventeen days to dig a 55-foot-long tunnel that emerged in a nearby tobacco warehouse. On the night of February 9, 1864, 109 prisoners managed to escape through that tunnel and walk off into the town before the guards noticed something was amiss. Fifty-nine escapees would make it back to Union lines, forty-eight were recaptured, and two drowned in the James River. It was a massive blow to Confederate morale, and a psychological coup for the Union.

RIGHT & BELOW
Libby Prison, where, according to the Daily Richmond Enquirer, *soldiers were "huddled and jammed into every nook and corner."*

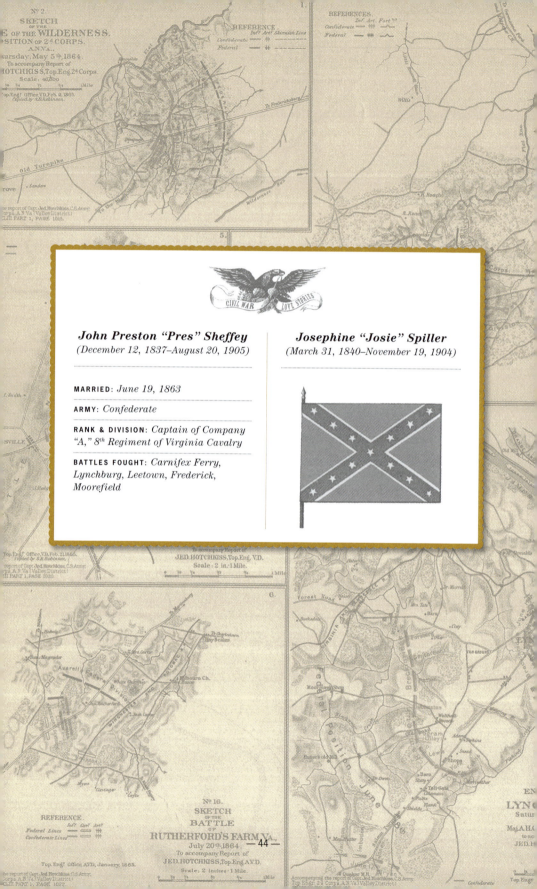

John Preston "Pres" Sheffey
(December 12, 1837–August 20, 1905)

MARRIED: *June 19, 1863*

ARMY: *Confederate*

RANK & DIVISION: *Captain of Company "A," 8ᵗʰ Regiment of Virginia Cavalry*

BATTLES FOUGHT: *Carnifex Ferry, Lynchburg, Leetown, Frederick, Moorefield*

Josephine "Josie" Spiller
(March 31, 1840–November 19, 1904)

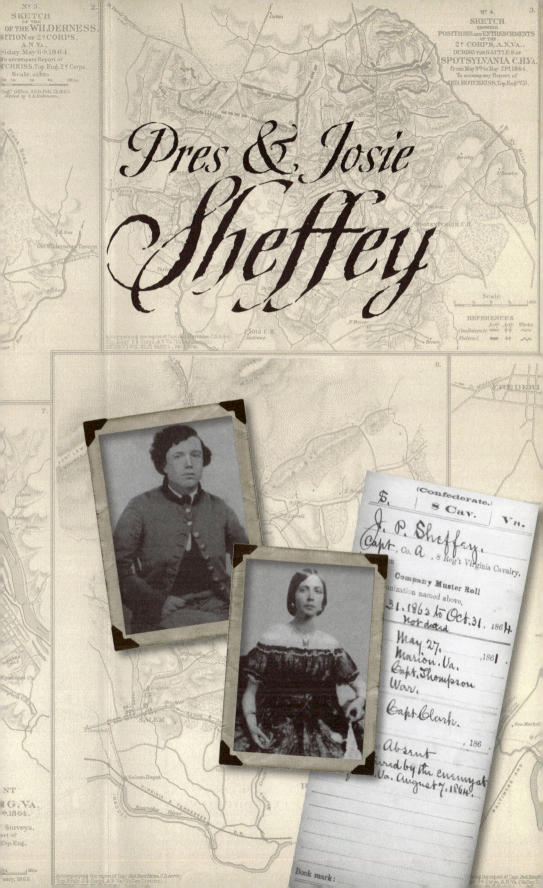

Marion Smyth Co. Va
April 8th 1861

Miss Josie

I am very — very grate-
ful to you for the two kindly and
beautiful letters you have written
to me. But I feel that I have,
as it were, stolen them from you,
that I have drawn you into this
correspondence, almost, if not
altogether against your
consent. I wish it were not
so. But I will do nothing
calculated in the slightest degree
to offend you. I have therefore
apologised for the two letters
I have written; and I ought
to ask your forgiveness for this
one in almost every sentence
for it is thoroughly uncalled for
by anything I can find in either of

Pres Sheffey wooed the love of his life, Josie, in beautifully written letters, full of quotations from Shakespeare and other literary allusions. But it was only after he began the strategy of mentioning the charms of other girls that Josie finally agreed to set their wedding date.

The first link between the Sheffey and Spiller families was a tragic one. A man named James Austin Graham wanted to marry one of Josie Spiller's older sisters but her father, William Spiller, refused to give permission. One night in 1855, James Graham shot and killed William Spiller in a bar, and when the case came to court, James White Sheffey, Pres's father, was the prosecuting attorney. The killer was committed to an asylum for the insane.

Pres Sheffey didn't meet the young, fatherless Josie until 1857, when he was in his final year at Emory & Henry College, in Emory, Virginia, and she was elected "Queen of Love and Beauty" in her home town of Wytheville. Her family owned property and general stores in the area, so were still wealthy even without her father at the helm. She was pretty and well-educated, with a diploma from William D. Roedel's Seminary for Girls, and Pres fell head over heels in love with her. He courted her, but in vain: she rejected his suit, and he left the area disappointed, to spend two years studying law at the University of Virginia, in Charlottesville.

On his admission to the bar, Pres joined his father's law practice in Marion, Virginia. But he couldn't forget his old flame and, in March 1861, in an attempt to rekindle their relationship, he wrote her a letter: "No reminiscences of the past do I better love to recall than the memory of that correspondence, short-lived & ill-fated though it prove to be." She replied to him with a brief note, so he wrote again, this time a longer letter, rewarded with yet another note from her. Encouraged, he launched into full

"No reminiscences of the past do I better love to recall than the memory of that correspondence, short-lived & ill-fated though it prove to be."

OPPOSITE
Writing in April 1861, Pres apologizes for drawing Josie back into correspondence with him, saying, "I will do nothing calculated in the slightest degree to offend you."

"*There is nothing honourable and possible
I would not dare, to gain your love.*"

courtship, writing, "There is nothing honourable and possible I would not dare, to gain your love." He told her he had tried without success to get over the "haunting passion" of his youth, and begged her to accept now the love she had rejected when they were both younger.

Within a few weeks Pres had asked her to marry him and, while she was swayed by his romantic eloquence and his ardent pursuit, she hesitated. He wanted to marry before he went off to fight in the war, but she refused to set a date, and in May she "struck gloom" into his heart by suggesting "an indefinite postponement."

If she loved him, why delay? The reason she gave was that the separations made necessary by war would be harder to bear once they were married. Perhaps Josie found it difficult to make such a decision without a father to advise her. Maybe the real reason for her procrastination was that, having lost her father at the age of fifteen, she was scared to commit herself to someone who was heading off to battle. Perhaps she simply couldn't face the heartache of becoming a young widow.

The campaign of persuasion

Pres was a passionate believer in Secession and helped to organize a local cavalry unit, the Smyth Dragoons, which would become part of the 8th Virginia Cavalry. From May to July 1861, they were training close to Wytheville, and Pres was able to spend time with Josie, but as Union forces advanced into western Virginia they were driven south, while she stayed behind in Wytheville with her family.

Two local Confederate generals, Henry A. Wise and John B. Floyd, disagreed over strategy and failed to support each other, making a number of costly blunders. Pres had seen a few skirmishes before, in September 1861, becoming involved in his first proper battle, at Carnifex Ferry—a combat which led to an embarrassing Confederate retreat, for which Floyd and Wise blamed each

POSTAL DELIVERIES

Both the Confederate and the Union army chiefs knew that getting word from home was crucial for their troops' morale, and they assigned men to the task of collecting and delivering soldiers' mail. The Confederate government established its own post office department as early as February 1861, and by June the price of a stamp for a letter traveling up to 500 miles had been set at 5 cents. The United States Post Office Department redesigned its postage stamps and charged 3 cents for sending a letter up to 3,000 miles, but soldiers didn't have to pay if they wrote "Soldier's letter" on the front of the envelope. Horse-drawn mail wagons carried letters over shorter distances, while the railroad was used for longer ones, but both were subject to disruption when bridges were destroyed or battles got in the way. Pres Sheffey mentions that his unit captured a mail sack and had themselves "a merry time" laughing over the endearments in the Yankees' love letters to girlfriends back home.

other. Pres was distantly related to Floyd but rapidly became disillusioned with his tactics, doubting the generals would achieve anything while they remained at loggerheads. His unit was assigned to guarding the Virginia and Tennessee Railroad in the winter of 1861–62, and he was also present during skirmishes at Princeton and Lewisburg, before taking part in raids against Union troops, though none of these were major battles. Indeed, stuck in his small corner of the fighting, Pres could only guess at what was happening with the rest of the war.

He kept up his letter-writing campaign, endeavoring to persuade Josie to set a date while frequently complaining that he was not getting many letters back from her: "I . . . will surrender myself to the Yankees or incurable blues within a fortnight if you don't write," he told her, but then, when she did, he accused her of writing coldly, as a friend rather than a lover. In May 1862, he sounded as though he was losing his patience when he wrote that if she was not willing to share his lot, it must mean that she did not love him. He went home on leave to discuss the situation with her and, after that, he began to mention other young ladies in his letters, in such flattering detail that it can only have been a campaign designed to make Josie jealous. Miss Emma Brown had a complexion "as fair as the most polished Parisian;" Miss Bettie Caperton was "graceful in face" and "a clever girl;" Miss Harriet Krebs was "a woman that a man might accidentally fall in love with."

BELOW
*The Wytheville Valley:
it is claimed that a
woman named Molly
Tines rode 40 miles
across these mountains
to warn the people
of Wytheville the day
before Union raiders
struck in July 1863.*

Still Josie held out. Back in Wytheville, she wrote that she was having a gay time with a younger set, taking part in tableaux (in which she and her friends dressed up to create a scene or picture) and other entertainments. Was this just reciprocation for his teasing? Did she still have misgivings about marrying a soldier? In March 1863, Pres wrote a heartfelt letter about his deep and unchanging love for her, saying the years that had passed showed that it was "no ordinary affection." Were she to be struck deaf, dumb, or blind, or to become "an object hideous to all other eyes," still to him she would be beautiful and her love essential to his happiness.

ABOVE
Men of the 1st Virginia Cavalry wore a state-seal belt plate and carried cavalry swords as well as revolvers.

At last, after more than two years of passionate, persuasive letters, Josie was moved to set a wedding date of June 9, 1863, and the couple invited as many of their friends and family as could make it to celebrate the festivities in Wytheville. Finally, instead of addressing his letters to "Dear Josie," Pres could write to "My dear wife."

A wounded enemy soldier

Pres had almost three weeks with his bride before he returned to his unit on June 29. A month after their wedding, on July 18, 1863, he was horrified to hear that Josie's home town of Wytheville had been attacked by Union forces, who were targeting the Virginia and Tennessee Railroad. Home guards defended the town but initial reports suggested that many houses had been burned and civilian lives lost. Pres was beside himself with worry until he got news that Josie was unharmed and the damage less serious than he'd feared. The Unionists were forced to retreat, leaving behind some wounded men, among them Colonel William H. Powell of the 2nd West Virginia Cavalry. Josie's mother, Susan Spiller, took pity on the injured colonel and hid him in a local hotel where, along with two other local women, she tended to his wounds. Once he was sufficiently recovered, she handed him over to the Confederate authorities to be treated as a prisoner of war, and six months later he was part of a prisoner exchange which returned him to his unit. Pres wasn't best pleased when he heard his wife's family had been harboring one of the enemy who were "murdering" his comrades on the battlefield, but in fact it would turn out to be much to his advantage a year later.

During the next months, Pres was not able to get leave to visit Josie, but kept writing long, news-filled letters describing life in the different army camps where he stayed. In August 1863, he was afflicted with a nasty eye disease that created a large, suppurating growth in the corner of one eye. He told Josie not to worry, but it continued to bother him for months. An operation to drain the abscess was discussed but inevitably there was a shortage of surgeons with the experience to carry it out, and eventually it cleared up by itself.

Early in 1864, Pres became a judge advocate engaged in presiding over courts-martial, work he found boring and dispiriting. He wrote wearily to Josie, quoting Shakespeare in stating that someday, "the winter of our discontent will be made glorious summer."

Back home in Virginia, women were terrified that their houses would be occupied by Union forces. Pres's sister Ellen wrote to Josie from Marion, Virginia, saying that they were discussing what to do with their furniture, silver, and jewelry, to prevent them from falling into the hands of the enemy. Josie must have been relieved when Pres was allowed home on leave for a few weeks in May 1864, but after that the 8th Virginia headed into the fighting around the Shenandoah Valley, and were engaged in battles at Lynchburg, Virginia, Leetown, West Virginia, and Frederick, Maryland. At the end of July, they set up camp near Moorefield, West Virginia, and were still in their beds on the morning of August 7 when Union forces launched a surprise attack. Of almost 2,000 men in the 8th Virginia, 420 were captured, with Pres among them. He was sent to Camp Chase, Ohio, a prisoner-of-war camp, where he would spend the next six months.

In many ways his capture was a blessing. At least he was safe there, away from the slaughter that awaited thousands of other Confederate soldiers as the Union Army advanced on Richmond and the war entered its closing stages. Still, Josie must have been frantic with worry, as news filtered out about inhumane conditions in prisoner-of-war camps.

DESERTERS

Desertion was a common problem for both armies, and there were many causes: concern for families back home and lack of leave of absence; shortage of food and basic amenities; and self-preservation, as men saw their friends and neighbors fall on the battlefield. In the later years of the war, desertion became endemic among Confederate soldiers—more than one in seven deserted—as pessimism spread about the eventual outcome of the fighting. General Robert E. Lee called for severe punishments for deserters, including whipping, branding, and even hanging. Pres Sheffey hated death sentences being passed on deserters, writing to Josie, "I hope . . . that a long period may elapse before such severity will again be necessary in our Brigade." Some who had given up hope of Confederate victory chose other paths apart from desertion, and there were many instances of self-inflicted gunshot wounds, surreptitious surrender to Union lines at night, and even suicide.

BELOW

In the first years of the war, deserters were treated with leniency, but from 1863 onward they were often executed to act as a deterrent to others considering the same course of action.

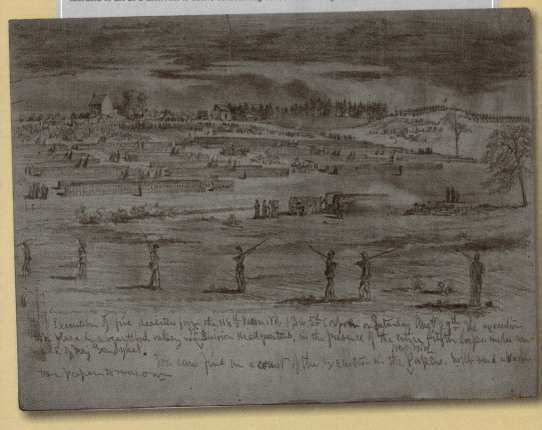

SPIES

When Pres wrote to Josie of military matters, he warned her to beware of imparting information to anyone who might turn out to be a spy. In fact, it was a war in which generals were often careless about discussing their plans, and several women were arrested for spying. A Washington socialite called Rose O'Neal Greenhow, who was friends with many military men, passed information to Confederate general Beauregard that he credited as helping him to win the Battle of First Bull Run. Belle Boyd of Martinsburg, Virginia, spied for Stonewall Jackson during the Shenandoah Valley campaign. For the Union side, General Ulysses S. Grant credited Elizabeth Van Lew with giving him the best information he received from inside Richmond during 1864–65. She even persuaded President Jefferson Davis's wife's maid to become part of her hugely successful spy ring.

ABOVE
Rose O'Neal Greenhow, Confederate spy.

Homeward bound

When Colonel William Powell, the Union officer Josie's mother had nursed, heard of Pres Sheffey's capture, he asked that the Confederate captain receive special treatment during his stay at Camp Chase. Accordingly, Pres was given a room in the officers' section of the barracks, where he was able to play games such as chess and backgammon, to read books and newspapers, and to take part in debates with a debating society in which, he wrote, "eloquence is dispersed with." He was allowed to write two letters a week, and he did receive some letters from Josie, although not as many as he would have wished; postal services between North and South had been banned early in the war, though prisoners' letters were sometimes exchanged under a flag of truce.

In the rest of the camp, other prisoners were not so lucky. While Camp Chase was by no means among the worst of the Civil War prisons, there was certainly poor sanitation and insufficient food. In such circumstances it was hardly surprising that a smallpox epidemic caused nearly 3,000 deaths in the second half of 1864, though the only ailment to affect Pres was an infection at the site of the smallpox vaccination he was given.

Immediately after his capture, Pres's lawyer father had approached James A. Seddon, the Confederate secretary of war, asking him to intervene and help secure the release of his son. It's unclear whether it was Seddon's influence or whether Colonel Powell pulled some strings, but in February 1865 Pres was chosen to be part of a prisoner exchange program. First he was transferred to the camp at Point Lookout, Maryland, to be exchanged for a Union officer of the same rank, before being taken by boat to Richmond. Pres was back at home with his

ABOVE
Camp Chase was a recruitment and training base for Union soldiers as well as a prison camp. During the course of the war, more than 2,000 Confederate prisoners died there.

beloved wife well before General Robert E. Lee surrendered at Appomattox Court House in April.

After the war, Pres's father helped him take over a law practice and buy a house in Marion, Virginia, with six large rooms and three-quarters of an acre of garden. Josie had wanted to stay near her family in Wytheville, but Pres had to be near his office, and spent the summer of 1865 repairing some fire damage and having their new home fitted out with a "neat kitchen." In the following years, he and Josie had five daughters and two sons, and Pres became a well-respected attorney in the town. In January 1895, at the age of fifty-eight, he was appointed a judge in the Virginia legislature, a position he held for nine years.

In February 1904, Pres retired to spend more time with Josie, who had been suffering ill health, but was devastated when she died in November that year, at the age of sixty-four. Just nine months later, the grieving Pres followed her to the grave and was buried by her side. There had never been any other woman for him, from the moment he first set eyes on her back when he was a nineteen-year-old student and she was the seventeen-year-old Wytheville "Queen of Love and Beauty." It took him over two years' persistence and much paper and ink, but the "strange passion" which began in his boyhood did finally bring him the "infinite happiness" he had always known it would.

> . . . the "strange passion" which began in his boyhood did finally bring him the "infinite happiness" he had always known it would.

FORT V
CHARGE OF
JULY

David Andrew Demus
(1839–1871[1])

MARRIED: *1860*

ARMY: *Union*

RANK & REGIMENT: *Private in Company K, 54th Massachusetts Volunteer Infantry*

BATTLES FOUGHT OR PRESENT AT: *Grimball's Landing, Fort Wagner, Olustee, Honey Hill, Boykin's Mill*

[1]David Demus was born 1838–40, and died 1870–2

Mary Jane Christy
(November 1841–after 1880)

nt's Creek

GNER
TH MASS
863.
4th Mass

Hacking column;
...ration when pas
...d the oblique at
...e curtain

OR WAGNER

WAGNER

David & Mary Demus

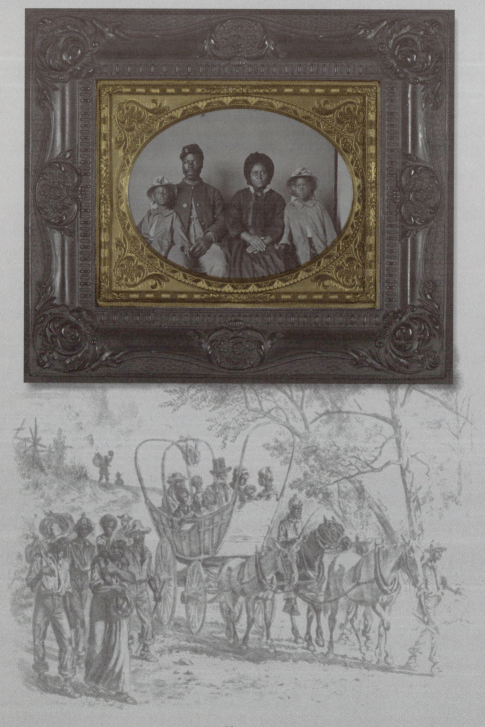

As an African-American, David Demus was incredibly proud to serve in one of the first African-American units of the Civil War, but he and his wife Mary Jane found their separation very difficult—especially when he was injured and then heard that the fighting had reached her doorstep back home.

The Demus and Christy families lived in the same small community in Mercersburg, Franklin County, Pennsylvania, so David and Mary Jane grew up knowing each other. There were nearly 400 African-American or mixed-race citizens in Mercersburg at the time, most of them born there. Slavery had been widespread in Pennsylvania in the 18th century, so some townspeople were ancestors of those slaves, while others were freed slaves who had crossed the border from the South. Mary Jane's father owned his own small farm, where she lived with him and her four brothers, and when she married her childhood sweetheart, David Demus, in 1860, he moved in immediately. It must have been hard work for her looking after all those men.

For almost the first two years of the Civil War, African-Americans were not allowed to enlist. The idea of giving them guns was anathema to many less enlightened folk in the North, who believed they would not make good soldiers. When more manpower was needed and African-American enlistment began, Confederate president Jefferson Davis issued a proclamation saying that any captured African-American soldiers could be sentenced to death or returned to slavery, which it was thought would act as a deterrent for those who were considering enlistment. But in March 1863, when Massachusetts governor John A. Andrew authorized the formation of an African-American regiment, the 54th Massachusetts, the response was overwhelming. Recruiters encountered unmitigated enthusiasm in areas with a strong African-American community, and in Mercersburg ten men enlisted on the April 22, 1863—three of Mary Jane's brothers, her husband, and his two brothers among them. David was proud to be able to serve: "The reason I come," he wrote to Mary Jane later, "was because I

"I thought it a big thing to be a soldier."

OPPOSITE TOP
A soldier's wife and two daughters wear their Sunday best to be photographed with him in his Union uniform.

OPPOSITE BOTTOM
African Americans seek refuge with Union troops near Culpeper Court House, Virginia.

SOLDIERS' PAY

Although the 54th had been promised a wage of $13 a month, the same as white soldiers, they were told in June 1863 that this would be just $10 a month, from which $3 would be deducted for their clothing. Colonel Shaw, their regimental commander, protested strongly, as did his successor Colonel Hallowell. Both men and officers refused to accept their wages, even though it caused hardship for them and their families. In April, a congressional bill gave equal pay to soldiers who were free men as of that month, but it didn't apply to the whole 54th. Finally, on September 28, 1864, the men of the 54th, who by that time had been serving for eighteen months, were given pay equal to that of their white comrades, alongside a guarantee that this would also be backdated.

RIGHT
Every African-American who enlisted was aware that he had an uphill struggle to convince his white comrades he was trustworthy and fit for battle.

thought it a big thing to be a soldier." There were financial incentives, too: they were offered a $50 bounty on enlisting, $13 a month pay (the same as white soldiers), and $8 a month for their families back home.

Their motives for enlisting, however, were not the same as those of their white comrades. Rather than fighting to preserve the Union, they sought to end slavery and to try to earn their right to United States citizenship at a time when Massachusetts was still the only state in which African-American men had full voting rights. The war was well underway by the time the 54th Regiment was formed, and so these new soldiers would have been familiar with reports of the carnage at battles such as Shiloh and Antietam, and must have known there was a strong chance they wouldn't all return. Joining up was a big risk.

Proving themselves

The 54th trained at Camp Meigs near Boston, under their white commander Colonel Robert Gould Shaw, and David began writing to Mary Jane soon after they arrived. His letters were formal, always beginning, "I take my Pen in hand to inform you that I am well at Present." It's clear that he was not accustomed to letter-writing, but his emotion couldn't help but shine through these moments of formality: "how happy I would be to see your Dear little face again," he wrote on one occasion, and on another, "how happy I would feel and I could kiss your Dear rosy lips Whenever I felt like it." Her letters were briefer than his and somewhat apologetic—"please to excuse the bad writing and the mistake"—but, again, her love was evident, as she worried about his safety, concluding that "all we can do is put our trust in god."

"how happy I would be to see your Dear little face again,"

At the end of May 1863, with basic training finished, the 54th marched past cheering crowds in Boston, and boarded steamships to take them down to the islands off the coast of Georgia. It was plantation country, and although the wealthy plantation owners had fled, there was plenty for them to loot when they were ordered to raid the town of Darien. David wrote to Mary that they got "a great deal of furniture and some sheep and cattle hogs and chickens." After taking what they wanted, they set fire to the town. But David doesn't seem to have regarded this as "revenge" on slave owners; rather, he was simply pleased by the welcome additions to their rations.

In late June 1863, news reached the regiment that the Confederates had launched a raid close to David's home in Franklin County, and were rounding up African-American people, even those born and raised on free soil, to take them into slavery.

ABOVE
An African-American soldier. There were 166 regiments of United States Colored Troops (U.S.C.T.) by the war's end. At first they were put to manual labor, but once they'd proved their courage they were often used in battle.

The assault on Fort Wagner on July 16, 1863, was an ill-judged attempt to capture a heavily fortified position. Afterwards, the beach was covered in Union dead.

It was a short-lived attack of just a few days, and his wife and family were unaffected, but it must have been heart-wrenching for David to contemplate Mary Jane being in the firing line when he was too far away to protect her.

Some African-American troops in other regiments were kept from the front line and given manual jobs such as digging trenches or guarding railroads, but the 54th saw action soon after their arrival in Georgia. There was a skirmish on James Island on July 16, then on the 18th Colonel Shaw led them in an assault on Fort Wagner, which was defended by 1,200 Confederate troops and fourteen cannons. The 54th were generally agreed to have fought with great courage, but this fruitless battle cost 1,515 Union casualties, leaving Colonel Shaw dead and David Demus with a fractured skull from being shot in the head.

It was a horrific wound. The camp doctor said it would never heal, and simply left the skin to grow over. Afterwards, David suffered horrible recurring headaches and was unable to be around any noise or out in the hot sun; he hoped in vain that

he might be sent home to recuperate. In October, he wrote to
Mary Jane that while washing his head, he felt something loose
within the wound and pulled out a piece of skull, which made his
head sore again.

Throughout this period, her letters were a lifeline: "if you know
how glad I was when I got that [letter] why you would have laughed,"
he wrote. But he also worried that his head was so swollen and
disfigured, she might not recognize him when she saw him again.

The harsh realities of wartime

Part of the appeal of enlisting had undoubtedly been the pay a
man could hope to receive, but when the men of the 54th heard
they were being paid less than white soldiers, they refused to
accept their pay on principle, and fought regardless. It was a
difficult decision for many, made more so for David when, in
November 1863, he heard that Mary Jane had been out husking
corn in the fields to earn some money. He wrote sharply, "I don't
want to hear of you going in the field any more," although two
days later he wrote to apologize for his tone. Later she went to

work for a neighbor, and though
David wished she need not,
he could do nothing about it.
When it came to financial
matters, Mary Jane ruled the
household. In spring 1865
they had quite an argument
after he borrowed money from
her brother Jacob and "tried
to make himself big," the
accusation Mary Jane leveled
at him in one letter. For
several weeks, her letters
brought him "nothing but
abuse" and he was so alarmed
that he wrote he would be
"Sorry if it would cause you
and I to part." What he did
with the money he borrowed
is unknown, but it certainly
made Mary Jane angry.

BELOW
*David's injury is listed
on the casualty sheet,
without any detail.
He is simply described
as "Wounded."*

By the winter of 1863–64, the company rations that had initially been plentiful had dried up, and his Christmas dinner consisted of "a tin of coffee and 2 pieces of hard tack." Hard tack was a tough biscuit that should be soaked in water before eating, but he told Mary Jane that you could "soak them in water for 8 Weeks and tramp on them and maybe you Can see a little mark in them . . . [if you] look very Close." He was demoralized after watching a deserter facing the firing squad in December 1863, and then, at the Battle of Olustee in Florida in February 1864, the regiment lost a good many men—Mary Jane's brother William was killed and her brother Joseph was wounded in the head. She reacted with disbelief, writing many times to ask David if he was sure, and that there hadn't been some mistake, but he assured her that he had checked with the man who was standing right next to William when he was hit.

After a year away from home, David's enthusiasm had faded, and he yearned to see his wife. He was delighted to hear from a

"I shall die a trying for our rights so that other that are born hereafter may live and enjoy a happy life."

friend, Wesley Krunkleton, that she had put on weight: "he told me that you Was that big and fat that you had to Come in the house side Ways or you Would fill up the door" he wrote, in what was considered a compliment for the day. He confessed that he himself wasn't as fat as he used to be, but in July 1864 he was made a clerk in the camp's provision stores, giving him plentiful access to food, besides which he even had a little money to buy tobacco. He was later made responsible for butchery when his headaches made it difficult for him to be on more active duty. In November he went home briefly on furlough, but he wrote immediately afterward that "if i had a known that it Would go so hard With me for to leave you Why i Would not a Come home till i Could a Come to stay."

And yet still David clung to the ideal for which he was fighting: "if it had Not a been for the Colored troops Why this awful war Would last for ten years to Come." He wrote it was "plane to see" that if African-American soldiers had not fought, then African-American people would not be entitled to claim full citizenship. He considered "us Colard men" the cause of "this Ofel [awful] Rebelon." Mary Jane's brother Jacob stated it more plainly: "I shall die a trying for our rights so that other that are born hereafter may live and enjoy a happy life."

The final year

In summer 1864, there was another Confederate raid on Franklin County, which must have been terrifying for Mary Jane. David wrote he was glad that she "got of safe," but Jacob was angered that the white men of the town had done nothing to stop the Confederate soldiers. He was confident that his company of 80 soldiers "can Wipe the best 200 rebels that they can fetch to us."

The symbolism of free African-American men fighting white slave owners was not lost on anyone. When the 54th arrived in Carolina in 1863, the *Charleston Mercury* deplored the fact that "our slaves are to be made equals in our own country, fighting against us." The 54th was briefly part of General Sherman's Savannah Campaign, at the Battle of Honey Hill, and they embraced the strategy of burning houses, pillaging crops, and destroying railroads with vigor. After the peace was declared in April 1865, they marched out from Georgetown, South Carolina, "to hunt the Johneys [Confederate soldiers]," and according to Mary Jane's brother Joseph, they "kild a grate meney of them." As they went, they freed over 4,000 slaves, who followed them in a long line stretching back down the road,

ENTERTAINMENTS IN CAMP

David wrote to Mary Jane on November 25, 1863, that they had celebrated Thanksgiving and "it Was the best day that We ever had since i left home." The festivities included a blindfold sack race and a ball game, as well as a greasy-pole competition. The prize, at the top of the pole, was a pair of pants with $13 in the pocket—a month's wages for a white soldier, and well worth having. Greasy-pole competitions were usually set up by the wealthy so they could enjoy the sight of poor folk slithering and sliding around. Servant girls might try it for the chance of a pretty new dress, while other common prizes included legs of ham or mutton. Experienced greasy-pole climbers would wait until a few had gone first and removed the surface layer of grease. They would also wear a little sack of ashes around their waist, which they could use to make the pole less slippery.

ABOVE
Greasy pole competitions were popular in the 1860s.

SHERMAN'S MARCH TO THE SEA

On November 15, 1864, Union major general William Tecumseh Sherman led his army out of Atlanta to march the 300 miles to Savannah on the coast, deliberately pursuing a strategy of destruction along the way. "The crueller it is," he reasoned, "the sooner it [the war] will be over." His men burned mills, private houses, and cotton gins (machines for separating cotton fibers from the seeds) and pulled up railroad tracks, which they heated over fires and twisted into what were known as "Sherman's neckties." He had no supply lines behind him, so his 62,000 men had to forage for food as they went, but they met only pockets of resistance, and occasionally other units, such as the 54th, came to assist. On arrival in Savannah on December 21, Sherman captured the port, then sent a telegram to President Lincoln: "I beg to present you as a Christmas gift the City of Savannah." The campaign remains controversial for the $100 million of damage caused to the infrastructure of the South, and the fact that civilians were specifically targeted.

and Joseph wrote that it "was one of the greatest sights that I ever seen." Jacob wrote to describe the surrendering Confederate soldiers: "a great many men that did belong to the Rebel army in Charleston City now it goes very hard with them to give away under us colored soldiers but we knock them out of our way."

David just wanted to get home. He hoped that once he had repaid the money he had borrowed during the war, he would still have enough for them to buy a house of their own. "How happy it will Be to Me to get home to stay with you for i am tired," he wrote. In fact, his medical discharge papers show that he was still suffering the after-effects of his head wound, with headaches and a "morbid sensitivity to the sun."

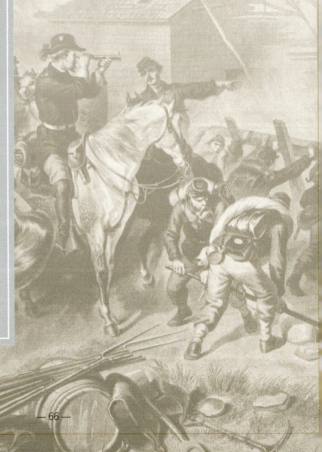

On his return to Mercersburg, David took
work as a farmhand on a farm owned by
James and Mary Witherspoon, where he had
worked before joining Mary Jane's father's
farm. But the long happy family life he
dreamed of with Mary Jane wasn't to be.
He died between five and seven years later,
while still in his early thirties, with his injury
a likely contributing factor. Mary Jane married again, to Wesley
Krunkleton, one of the other volunteers from Mercersburg who
signed up for the 54th Massachusetts, the man who told David that
she had got fat while he was away at war. But she must always
have been proud of her first husband, and she kept the letters he
had sent her, in which he had so beautifully expressed his hope
that he would survive to live with her again: "What a happy time
we will have . . . I will talk a mile."

> "*What a happy time
> we will have . . .
> I will talk a mile.*"

BELOW
*Sherman's soldiers
destroyed railroad
tracks and telegraph
poles, wiping out the
infrastructure of the
Southern economy for
decades to come.*

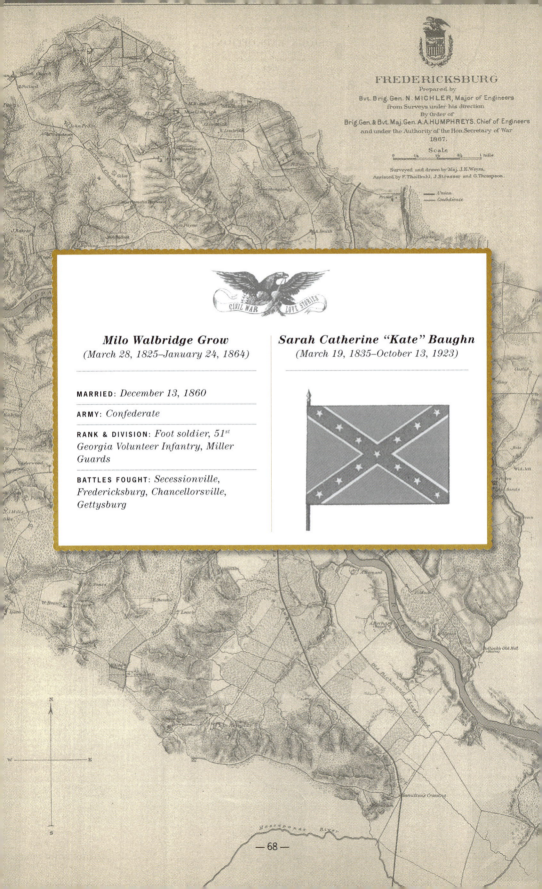

Milo Walbridge Grow
(March 28, 1825–January 24, 1864)

MARRIED: *December 13, 1860*

ARMY: *Confederate*

RANK & DIVISION: *Foot soldier, 51st Georgia Volunteer Infantry, Miller Guards*

BATTLES FOUGHT: *Secessionville, Fredericksburg, Chancellorsville, Gettysburg*

Sarah Catherine "Kate" Baughn
(March 19, 1835–October 13, 1923)

Milo & Kate Grow

Camp Paris March 18th 1862

My dear Sallie   I hasten to write to you by the
first opportunity, after my arrival here.
We arrived here on the morning following the day
on which your father left us in Albany
riding all night. The cars were very
ride was not very pleasant. We are e——
here with four or five thousand oth——
little tents which are three breadths of —
in length and about two in breadth ea——
The bottom of them is covered with —
and our blankets &c are packed —
which with the camp chest forms —
furniture. We drew from the gov——
tin pans like our milk pans —
bucket which is all we have alo——
We are entitled to more but th——
they have not got them. The cooking —
easy for us at any time becomes very tro——
with only these implements. We drew yesterday a
hand full of salt another of sugar a little coffee
and rice and meal and beef and a little bacon
and some soap and half a candle. Our tents are
scattered for two miles along the Rail Road.

Milo Grow came from New England but fell in love with a Southern woman and made his home in the South. After war was declared, he found himself under pressure to fight for a cause he didn't believe in and a land that wasn't his own.

Milo Grow was an intellectual who loved poetry and astronomy, history and geometry, classics and music. He grew up in Vermont and studied at Dartmouth College in Hanover, New Hampshire, where he would have been steeped in the new liberalism of the era. He would almost certainly have read Emerson's Essays and Thoreau's *Walden*, each of them in their own way questioning what it means to live a good life.

In 1853, at the age of twenty-eight, Milo moved to Georgia, where he opened his own school in Albany, teaching youngsters arithmetic, reading, philosophy, Greek, and Latin. According to his family, he was opposed to the slave trade, yet he set up home in a state where a quarter of the population owned at least one slave and some large plantation owners kept hundreds. In neighboring Alabama, it was a crime even to speak out against slavery, so Milo probably kept his opinions to himself as he made friends in the Albany area. Eventually, he met and fell in love with a lively, intelligent Florida woman named Sarah Catherine Baughn, known as Kate, who was ten years his junior.

Milo and Kate married on the eve of Lincoln's inauguration, and their son Roy (known as Lee, Leroy, and Leetle Lee) was born ten months later in October 1861—by which time the Civil War had been raging for six months. Milo faced an impossible dilemma. He didn't support Secession and his birth family all lived in the North, but he had made a life for himself in the South, and now Kate and little Roy were the center of his universe. As 1861 progressed, he must have been under extreme pressure from his neighbors to declare where his loyalties lay. If he didn't sign up for the Confederate Army, Sarah could have been accused of harboring a Yankee; if he did, he would prove himself to his neighbors—and the $50 bonus that came with enlistment must also have been hard to overlook.

BELOW
The Confederate flag of Georgia, 1862. Georgia was one of the original seven states to secede from the Union.

WRITERS' VIEWS ON THE WAR

Walt Whitman, the father of American poetry and author of the revolutionary *Leaves of Grass*, visited his injured brother in hospital and was so moved by the appalling injuries and piles of amputated limbs that he volunteered to work as a nurse. He wrote about his experiences in an influential newspaper article entitled, "The Great Army of the Sick," published in 1863. Ralph Waldo Emerson gave lectures calling for the emancipation of slaves, saying, "They call slavery an institution; I call it destitution." Meanwhile, in the South, Samuel Clemens (who would later achieve fame as Mark Twain) served two weeks in the Confederate Missouri State Guard before deciding he'd had enough and prudently heading out to California for the duration of the war.

Walt Whitman: fierce critic of the war.

In March 1862, with his baby son just five months old, Milo volunteered for the Miller Guards, part of the 51st Georgia Volunteer Infantry, which he hoped would remain within the state and avoid any heavy fighting. Little did he suspect that his brigade would see action in some of the bloodiest battles of the entire war. When they heard of Milo's decision, his Northern relatives were horrified. His father, Silas Grow, died in August 1862, having changed his will so that his estate would no longer be inherited by his eldest son.

Poet on the front line

As soon as he arrived in Camp Davis, Milo began writing to Sarah, in letters that are full of poetry and brimming with love. He was delighted that she had decided to work as a teacher, to earn money and to keep herself busy: "Your spirit is certainly much superior, more heroic, than many who trifle away their time and pine because their husbands are in the war." He suggested topics she could read about for her lessons, and gave advice on teaching, singing, and arithmetic. He often called her Lyra, after the constellation in the skies that was said to be the source of all inspiration, or Lullie, his pet name for her.

Her letters have not survived, but we can sense her intelligence and her romantic spirit through his responses to them. She was enjoying John Bunyan's *Pilgrim's Progress*, and sent him a pressed flower, which moved him greatly. She enquired whether he was warm enough and eating properly. She sewed his coat, found fresh socks for him, and posted him food when she could. She described to him their baby son, whom he confessed to missing very much. He wrote back wistfully, "I dreamed I heard little Lee saying Pa to me the other night. He must have grown very much."

> "*Your spirit is certainly much superior, more heroic, than many who trifle away their time and pine because their husbands are in the war.*"

The 51ˢᵗ saw action for the first time on June 16, 1862, when Northern troops tried to storm the Confederate fort of Secessionville on James Island, South Carolina. Milo wrote to reassure Sarah that while his regiment was charged with defending certain key points, they had not been under fire. After the battle, Milo wandered among the bodies of Union soldiers and picked up a rucksack belonging to one. It was commonplace to rifle through the possessions of those who fell on the battlefield and help yourself to souvenirs. He found a letter among the possessions of a soldier called S.C. Spence of the 8ᵗʰ Michigan Regiment, which turned out to be from his wife, and Milo regretted that she would never receive a reply to it. Some of his fellow soldiers were tearing up their wives' letters so they didn't fall into enemy hands, but Milo said he always kept one or two of Sarah's on his person. He sent her a gift of S.C. Spence's butter knife and kept his tin cup for himself.

BELOW
Retreating armies were often unable to rescue their wounded men or bury the dead.

In December, Milo's brigade was once again in battle, this time to protect the town of Fredericksburg. He kept a diary and described in poetic detail the vision of that scenic town surrounded by grim death in the form of lines of troops waiting to open fire on each other. He wrote of the shelling that sounded like an oncoming tropical storm and made men fall forward in their ditches "like flocks of partridges," as well as the remarkable aurora borealis, which was seen right across the war zone that month, and which he described as reaching up to the heavens "in colors of yellow and red."

"*Your love and tenderness is the oasis of my life,*"

One thousand six hundred Union soldiers died after storming the well-held Confederate positions, and Milo describes one wounded Union soldier who lay not far from his line. The man occasionally tried to stir himself to get help but could not move far, so he crawled for a bit then stopped and wrapped his blanket more tightly around him. Some of Milo's fellow soldiers called

THE BATTLE OF GETTYSBURG.

out to commiserate with him and would have saved him if they could, but to step out into the open at that point would have made them targets themselves. Milo was overwhelmed by the horror of it all, and he focused on his memories of Kate to try and regain his peace of mind: "Your love and tenderness is the oasis of my life," he wrote to her.

Then, in May 1863, the 51st Georgia joined Robert E. Lee's Army of Northern Virginia and took part in its most dangerous action to date, the battle of Chancellorsville, which would see 577 of the 1,832 men in the company killed or wounded. By the time Major General Hooker's Union Army was forced to withdraw, there was a massive death toll on both sides, and Milo wrote that he was tired and weary of the war. He yearned to find a way to get home to his wife and son, but the fighting was now relentless. All leave was canceled, and there was nothing he could do but keep marching, and keep following orders.

Gettysburg

Fresh from victory at Chancellorsville, Confederate general Robert E. Lee marched his troops north to strike at the Army of the Potomac in their home territory of Pennsylvania. Union commander general John Buford made a stand on some hilly ridges west of the town of Gettysburg to try and hold off the enemy until reinforcements could arrive. His position gave his men a geographical advantage, but Confederate rifles were more accurate than the muskets with which many Union brigades still fought, and the Southerners made some headway.

Late in the afternoon of July 2, Milo's brigade was ordered to advance into an area known as the Wheatfield, crossing open ground towards Northern infantry, who were firing from behind the cover of rocks and trees. By evening, 6,000 men lay dead or wounded in that field, and Milo was among the wounded. There was no chance of collecting him and getting him to a Confederate field hospital. His brigade were still in action the following day, holding some woods at the edge of a ravine, until they were

THE REBEL YELL

As they charged into battle, Confederate forces uttered an unearthly cry known as the rebel yell. It is likely to have derived from the war cries of Native American tribes, although some suggest a Scottish origin. Each regiment had their own yell, the soldiers' voices mingling together in one prolonged cry in an attempt to intimidate the opposition. Historian Shelby Foote described it as, "a foxhunt yip mixed up with a kind of banshee squall." Colonel Keller Anderson considered it "a penetrating, rasping, blood-curdling, shrieking noise that could be heard for miles." "It was the ugliest sound that any mortal ever heard," wrote Ambrose Bierce, a Union lieutenant who would later achieve fame as a writer.

OPPOSITE
The name "Gettysburg" has become synonymous with slaughter on an unimaginable scale.

PRISONER-OF-WAR CAMPS

The most notorious wartime camp was Andersonville in southwest Georgia, where 32,000 Union prisoners were held in a 26-acre stockade with no shelter from the blazing summer heat. There was inadequate food and water, and poor sanitation. By the war's end, 12,912 inmates had been buried there and images of emaciated survivors shocked the nation. The camps run by both sides were inhumane, with facilities ranging from existing prisons to disused warehouses and stockades that were like cattle pens. Food and medical attention for soldiers were scarce by the latter stages of the war, and prisoners came last on the priority list. Of the 400,000 men held captive by either side during the conflict, it's estimated that 13 percent of them perished— more than twice the percentage who died on the battlefield.

ABOVE
Prisoners captured at Gettysburg were marched to the new prison at Point Lookout in Maryland.

RIGHT
Captured Confederate soldiers sit under guard, waiting to hear their fate.

ordered to retreat to the point from which their advance had
started. The brigade suffered 430 casualties out of the 1,200
men they had set out with.

On July 4, when Lee's troops retreated from Pennsylvania
in the pouring rain, they didn't have the manpower to take the
wounded along with them. Two thousand injured soldiers were
left behind, Milo among them. During the early stages of the war,
there were often prisoner swaps after battle, and that must have
been Milo's hope, but the system had been suspended in May
1863, mainly because the Confederates insisted on treating
captured African-American soldiers as runaway slaves. Any
injured soldiers who couldn't escape after Gettysburg were
therefore captured and treated as enemy combatants. The last
letter Kate received from Milo was dated May 23, 1863, and she
must have been frantic with worry when there was no word from
him after Gettysburg.

On August 1, a new prisoner-of-war camp was established at
Point Lookout in Maryland, on a peninsula where the Potomac
River runs out into Chesapeake Bay,
and it was here that Milo was taken.
There were no barracks, just flat
sandy ground where the prisoners
slept in tents, surrounded by a
15-foot-high fence. Most of the
prison guards were African-
American soldiers, and there was a
lot of animosity between them and
the Southern prisoners. At mealtimes, according to camp survivor
Charles T. Loehr, "Our rations were such as kept us permanently
on the edge of starvation . . . Four small crackers or a small loaf
of bread a day, and a cup full of dish-water, called pea soup,
horrible to taste." There were no proper sanitation facilities, and
the camp's few wells soon became contaminated, meaning that
freshwater, of which there was never enough, had to be imported.

> "*Our rations were such as kept us permanently on the edge of starvation.*"

The real problem came with the freezing winter. At high tide
waves lapped close to the tents, the ground was swampy, and the
cold excruciating. Firewood was issued to the prisoners, but only
enough for them to keep a fire burning for two hours out of every
twenty-four. They lay huddled in blankets, trying to keep dry, too
weak to get up and walk around.

Milo held out for as long as he could, but in the depths of winter he fell ill with diphtheria. He managed to get word to his family in the North and his younger brother David traveled down to Point Lookout to buy Milo's release. He found him desperately weak but still able to talk faintly. "Tell my wife that my only desire to live is for her and our little boy," he whispered. David was a Freemason and found other Masons among the prison officers who promised to give Milo the best of care while the paperwork for his release was sorted out. But three days later, on January 24, Milo passed away.

Once a lover, always one

After his death, Milo's family wrote to Kate to tell her what had happened, no doubt confirming her worst fears. In the months that followed, the grieving widow struck up a warm correspondence with Milo's sister Mila, who described to her the funeral they held for him, the hymns that were sung, and his burial place alongside his father in St. Johnsbury, Vermont. It would have been impossible to send the body to Kate, she explained; in fact, by the time it reached them it was so long after his death that they were no longer able to view it.

Kate wrote that she was living with one of her brothers and still teaching school, while looking after little Roy. She sent copies of

BACKGROUND
It is estimated that 14,000 Confederate prisoners died at Point Lookout before the end of the war.

OPPOSITE
A letter Milo sent from Camp Davis, expressing his hope that Kate and Roy would be able to visit him there. They never did.

the letters Milo had written to her during the war along with a
picture of his son, to which Mila replied, "His letters show that
his affection was all that a loving wife could wish." Milo's mother
sent a letter to Roy telling him that he looked like his daddy as
a boy, when his family nickname was Wabbie (from his middle
name, Walbridge, which Roy shared).

Kate also wrote a moving poem to her late husband, in which
she wishes that he rest easy without
concern for those he has left behind:
"Sleep on, unmindful of the tears/Of
her thou once called wife." She was in
deep mourning, and told her sister-in-
law in the North that she would never
remarry—a promise she kept for twelve
difficult years, during which time she
focused her energies on raising her son.

> "*His letters show that his affection was all that a loving wife could wish.*"

If ever she needed comfort, she could look back on Milo's
letters and know how very deeply she had been loved. Every
time she looked up at the stars, she must have remembered
him calling her Lyra, the source of inspiration. As he said so
pertinently, "once a lover, always one."

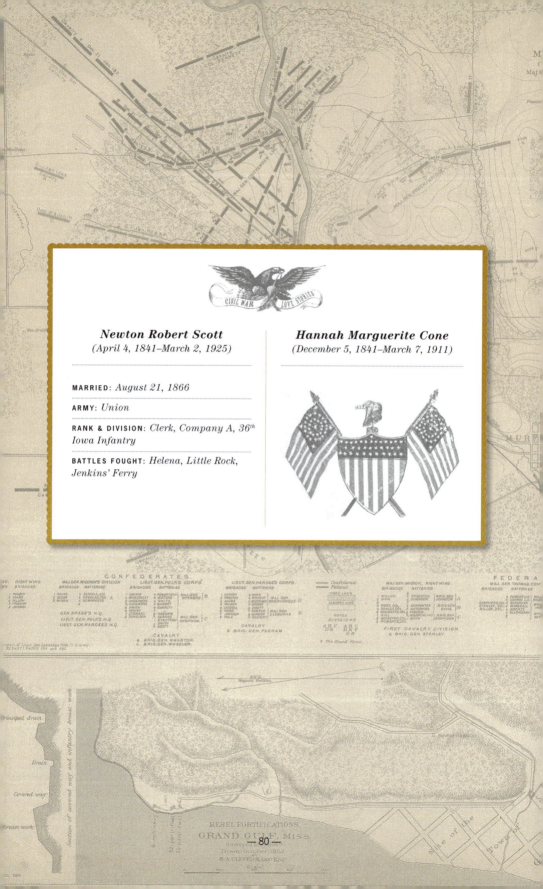

Newton Robert Scott
(April 4, 1841–March 2, 1925)

Hannah Marguerite Cone
(December 5, 1841–March 7, 1911)

MARRIED: *August 21, 1866*

ARMY: *Union*

RANK & DIVISION: *Clerk, Company A, 36th Iowa Infantry*

BATTLES FOUGHT: *Helena, Little Rock, Jenkins' Ferry*

Newton & Hannah Scott

Newton and Hannah were friends as teenagers and corresponded throughout his three years of war service, despite his having a sweetheart called Hattie. It seems that Hannah always felt more than friendship for him, though, and was happy to offer a shoulder to cry on when Hattie broke his heart.

Newton was born in Indiana but his parents moved to Albia, Iowa, when he was fourteen years old. Hannah Cone had been born in Saugamon, Illinois, but her family moved to Albia when she was two. She met Newton's sister, Amanda, as they attended the same Methodist church, and the two families became friends. When Newton was sent to war, Hannah wrote to him, reminding him, in an attempt to lift his spirits, of "the many happy hours that Your Self and I with Two others had Enjoyed" (the two others being her brother Will, known as WP, and Amanda).

Albia was a small town in Monroe County with a population of only 620 souls in the 1860 census, almost all of them families who had relocated from the east in search of good farming land. During the 1850s the railroads arrived, making it easier to transport goods to far-off markets, and Iowans became important suppliers of corn, beef, wheat, and pork to the Union Army during the war. Newton wasn't drawn to farming, though. He could read and write well, and managed to get work as a clerk with a railroad company. It was a decent job and it may have helped him to win the affections of Hattie Kester, a local girl who became his sweetheart when he was twenty years old. They weren't engaged, but he used to visit her two or three times a week, with his mother as chaperone, and he certainly considered her his girl, even though he knew she received visits from a "white-headed boy" as well as him.

Newton didn't leap to volunteer at the beginning of the Civil War. Like the majority of Iowans, he had voted for Abraham Lincoln, but the war wasn't in his state and didn't initially feel like his fight. However, by the summer of 1862, when Illinois congressman John A. McLernand began recruiting in Monroe County, he felt he had no option but to sign up, "until This Wicked

& God Forsaken Rebellion is Destroyed." He wrote scathingly of the "Cowardly Copperheads"—Democrats who spoke out against the war and advocated an immediate peace settlement. He might have been reluctant to fight in the beginning, but finally he enlisted, for a period of three years, in Company A of the 36th Iowa Infantry, and in October 1862 set off for camp. Would Hattie wait for him? He certainly hoped so.

Securing the Mississippi

Newton trained with his company at Camp Lincoln in Keokuk, Iowa, and it was from there that he wrote his first letter to Hannah, describing the bitter cold, with only one stove for eighty or ninety men to share. The sight of the many casualties must have been disheartening for a new recruit, and he wrote, "The numbers of Sick & Disabled Soldiers . . . would make your heart ache." He addressed her as "Dear Miss," and closed, "In friendship, love and Truth, I am Truly Yours." They were friends, and that was all.

> "*In friendship, love and Truth, I am Truly Yours.*"

Newton's unit sailed by steamer down the Mississippi to the Union garrison at Helena, Arkansas, continually at risk from the guerrilla bands which fired at them and injured two of their men. Arkansas had declared itself a Confederate state, but there were enough Union sympathizers that eleven Union regiments were formed from Arkansas volunteers. In Helena, Newton was glad to be appointed an ordnance sergeant, responsible for looking after the supplies, arms, and ammunition, because it meant he didn't have to take his turn on guard duty during the freezing-cold nights.

In June, he and Hannah's brother Will had their photographs taken by a camp photographer, and sent them back to Hannah. Newton asked that she have a picture taken of herself with his sister Amanda: "Have you Pictures taken Both on one Plate If you can get Good ones that way & If not Have them taken Single & Send to me." It was quite an intimate request for the era, and meant that she was in his thoughts. Although he complained that there weren't enough letters getting through, she seems to have been a regular correspondent and, when she finally sent a picture of herself, he responded that it was "verry Good."

On July 4, 1863, the Helena garrison was attacked by a Confederate force under General Holmes. On U.S. Navy gunboat *Tyler* there were "8 or ten guns . . . throwing Shells Amongst them thick as Hail," but the Confederates were still able to capture some positions, and there was some bloody hand-to-hand combat before the Union prevailed. Newton boasted to Hannah

BELOW
Ironclads were battleships covered in sloping steel plates, making it difficult to ram them or set them on fire.

PHOTOGRAPHERS

Photographic portraits were popular by the time of the Civil War, and some photographers set up tents in military camps where soldiers could get a tintype likeness on blackened iron that they could mail to their families or sweethearts back home. Photographic portrait cards (cartes de visite) were also extremely popular, with the subjects usually in full uniform and carrying their weapons. This was the first war in which photographers were able to take shots of battlefields, with the famous Civil War photographer Matthew Brady even hiring a team of men to go to the front line and document the scenes, using horse-drawn wagons as their darkrooms. His portfolio included portraits of many senior generals—mainly from the North, though some Confederate, too—and his men didn't shirk from photographing the carnage of battle. He invested over $100,000 of his own money, hoping that the U.S. government would buy the images from him after the war; when they didn't, he went bankrupt.

TOP
Sam A. Cooley, traveling photographer, plies his trade.

ABOVE
A Confederate soldier poses with canteen and cup around his neck.

RIGHT
Matthew Brady, the best-known Civil War photographer.

that they took 960 prisoners, including three colonels and three or four other field officers. There was much to celebrate as news came through that Vicksburg had surrendered to General Ulysses S. Grant on the same day, so that the war seemed to be going in the Unionists' favor on all fronts.

> 66
> *. . . give my love to all & Reserve a Share for your Self.*"

Hannah wrote describing an Independence Day celebration she had enjoyed with the "Sabbath school" where she taught, and he replied, somewhat sarcastically, "While you all was Having such Good times at Albia on the 4th . . . we was Shooting Rebels & the Bullets Came whistling around our Heads." There's an interesting change to the conclusion of the letter when he says, "give my love to all & Reserve a Share for your Self." His fondness for her was clearly growing. Doubtless he was feeling emotional after facing potential death in the line of battle. Did he sit by the campfire of an evening gazing at the tintype portrait of the woman who wrote such warm letters to him? It seems likely that she put his in a prominent place in her home back in Albia.

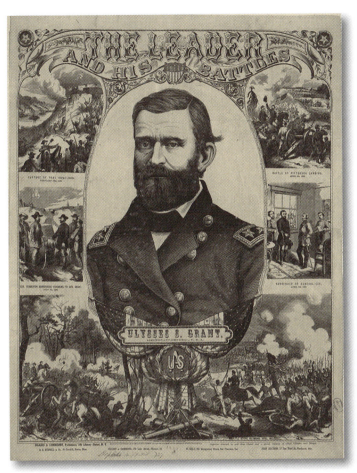

LEFT
*Ulysses S. Grant,
the victorious Civil
War general; in 1869
he would become the
18th President of
the United States.*

The war drags on

Newton's unit was involved in the capture of Little Rock, Arkansas, in September 1863, but over the winter his spirits sank. When he enlisted he had thought the fighting would continue perhaps a further fifteen months, but he was beginning to revise his estimate, wondering whether the war might last as long as five years, which for him would mean serving the full term of his three-year enlistment. Hannah asked if there was any chance he might come home on furlough and have some fun, but he replied that thirty days was the longest furlough given to anyone, and that by the time he had traveled home and back again there wouldn't be much time left to "enjoy the pleasures of friends."

NEW TYPES OF RIFLES

When the 36th Iowa men first joined up, they were issued with smoothbore muskets with bayonets, but these were eventually replaced by Enfield rifle muskets. In order to fire an Enfield, soldiers had to use their teeth to rip open a paper cartridge, which contained a Minié ball and a powder charge. They rammed both powder and ball down the barrel of the rifle using a ramrod, then placed a percussion cap in the firing mechanism. It sounds cumbersome, but with practice a man might reload and fire three times a minute. Common mistakes included leaving the ramrod in the barrel or forgetting to load powder; as ordnance clerk, Newton would have had to note any instances of damage to rifles, and provide replacements. By the later years of the war, repeat-loading weapons such as the Spencer rifle, which could fire twenty rounds a minute, and the Gatling gun, which could fire up to 200 rounds a minute, were coming into use.

RIGHT
A soldier holding a Sharps rifle: it was expensive but much more accurate than a musket.

In January 1864, Newton watched a Confederate spy, David O. Dodd, being hung after having been arrested with some important papers in his possession. The case obviously got under Newton's skin because he copied out the farewell letter Dodd left for his family telling them of his fate, and sent it to Hannah. Death was all around. He was heartened in February by the number of Confederates deserting the ranks and coming to Union lines to take an oath of allegiance. Prisoners of war were often released after swearing that they would "faithfully support, protect, and defend the Constitution of the United States." "There is Hardly a day But some come in & takes the oath," Newton wrote to Hannah, adding that "100 of them joined our army."

However, it wasn't all going their way. In April, the 36th Iowa were taken by surprise near Marks' Mills as they guarded a supply train, and three-quarters of them were either killed or forced to surrender, robbed of their possessions, and force-marched all the way to a prison camp in Tyler, Texas. Newton was spared this battle because he was ill at the time, but was nonetheless devastated by what

> "*My darling has long Forsaken me and Married and left me to mourn my life,*"

happened to his comrades. He blamed Lieutenant Colonel Francis Drake, who had been in charge at the time, writing to Hannah that it was the general opinion that "If our Brigade had have had another Commander in Place of Col Drake that Brigade would not have been Butchered & captured." Drake was wounded and captured at Marks' Mills but was part of a prisoner exchange a few weeks later, and returned to a hero's welcome in Iowa, despite the poor opinion in which his men held him.

There was another Union defeat at Jenkins' Ferry at the end of April, and summer saw Newton in a very low mood. "If Permited to live then I expect to Return Home & See the People & Eat Peaches," he wrote to Hannah in July 1864, but in the rest of the letter he listed all the friends who had died, or who were in their sick beds.

During this period Newton was working as a company clerk, with responsibility for keeping all the logs of men present or absent for duty, their physical appearance, clothing, pay, weapons, and any injuries or illnesses suffered. He was very conscious that at home in Albia life continued without him, and he sounded disapproving when he heard the news that his sister Amanda had got married. "Now she will have to Do as Best she Can," he wrote dryly, making clear that he didn't approve of her choice. With weddings on his mind, he asked after a mutual friend, Samantha Gillespie, and then summoned up the courage to ask about his sweetheart Hattie. He had his suspicions that she was not waiting patiently for him because of the dearth of letters from her, and also because, he said, "I Know that She is Tired of Single life Ere this time." In his next letter he wrote sarcastically to Hannah, "I expect that you have been loosing so much sleep attending these Oyster Suppers and the verry many Weddings."

BY STRANGE COINCIDENCE

The Civil War began and ended in the home of a man called Wilmer McLean, a Virginia grocer. On July 18, 1861, his farmhouse was being used as the headquarters of Confederate general Beauregard when Union artillery fired a cannonball, which dropped through the kitchen fireplace, marking the start of the First Battle of Bull Run. During the war, McLean moved to the village of Appomattox Court House. On April 8, 1865, a messenger knocked on his door, saying that Confederate general Robert E. Lee wanted to find a suitable place in which to surrender to Union general Ulysses S. Grant, and asking if they could use his home. The very next day the surrender took place there. "The war began in my front yard and ended in my parlor," he later said proudly.

Still he waited for an answer to his question, and the heart-breaking news came in May 1865, when Hannah told him that Hattie had married another. Perhaps she had done so some time earlier, and Hannah had decided to wait until after the Confederate surrender in April 1865 because she feared exacerbating Newton's low mood while the fighting continued. All the same, he gave the appearance of taking it badly. "My darling has long Forsaken me and Married and left me to mourn my life," he wrote, calling the news a "sad bereavement" and a "sudden shock." However, he doesn't sound either surprised or particularly heartbroken. The absence of any correspondence from Hattie must have told him long before that she had not had sufficient patience to wait three years for him.

But someone else had. There was a strong hint in Hannah's letter of May 1865, when she said that there was something she could not write but would tell him when he got home. Did she mean to declare her feelings for him? He begged her to write again soon and tell him "all the News and Particulars," but didn't seem to have a clue that there might be another girl back in Albia who was ready and willing to take Hattie's place.

The longest months

By spring 1865, Newton was counting the days until he could come home. He hoped he might be released after the surrender at Appomattox on April 12, but such hope was thwarted by the task he was given of taking oaths of allegiance from Confederate soldiers west of the Mississippi and north of the Arkansas River. In all, he was made to serve another five months after the surrender, only being discharged from the army on August 24, 1865.

Finally, Newton made his way back to Albia, where he soon realized that Hannah was interested in more than just friendship with him. Perhaps she confessed her feelings, or at least hinted in the strongest terms; at any rate, they began courting and were married a year later. They went on to have nine children together—five daughters and four sons—although one son died as an infant and one daughter at the age of eleven. Newton worked for almost forty years as a railway clerk,

> " ... *he soon realized that Hannah was interested in more than just friendship.*"

not retiring till he was seventy-two years old, and he helped to organize and raise funds for the building of a Methodist Episcopal Church in Murray, Iowa, where both he and Hannah were dedicated worshippers.

Had Newton not gone to war, might he have married Hattie Kester, the girl who was too impatient to wait three years for him? We'll never know. What is certain is the forty-five year marriage he enjoyed with a girl who made her way into his thoughts and his heart by writing to raise his spirits throughout the long war, and by waiting hopefully and faithfully for his return.

BELOW
Robert E. Lee and Ulysses S. Grant met face to face in Appomattox Court House to agree the terms of surrender. The Union proved more generous than Southerners had anticipated.

William "Keith" McKesson Blalock
(November 21, 1837–April 11, 1913)

MARRIED: *April 1861*

ARMY: *Confederate, then Union*

RANK & REGIMENT: *Sergeant, 26th North Carolina Infantry; recruiting officer and scout captain, 10th Michigan Cavalry*

BATTLES FOUGHT: *Dozens of skirmishes and bushwhacks but no major battles*

Sarah Malinda Pritchard Blalock
(March 10, 1842–March 9, 1903)

MARRIED: *April 1861*

ARMY: *Confederate, then Union*

RANK & REGIMENT: *Soldier, 26th North Carolina Infantry; scout and aide-de-camp, 10th Michigan Cavalry*

BATTLES FOUGHT: *Dozens of skirmishes and bushwhacks but no major battles*

Keith & Malinda Blalock

Malinda loved Keith so passionately that she couldn't bear to be parted from him when he enlisted for war—so she disguised herself as a man and signed up as well. During the war years, through injury and hardship, they were always at each other's side.

BELOW
*Keith Blalock
as a young man,
looking unusually
well-groomed,
with his stepfather
Austin Coffey.*

BELOW RIGHT
*Malinda Blalock
holding a photograph
of her husband.*

In the Blue Ridge Mountains of Northern Carolina, family was a revered institution that obliged you to revenge any wrongs inflicted on a relative, come what may. Boys were taught to stand up for themselves from a young age, learning to hunt, fish, and fight; girls were responsible for all the traditional domestic tasks, though they also had to learn to ride and shoot.

Keith and Malinda attended the same school, but, as he later told a friend, the first time he really noticed her was when a teacher hit her with a switch for talking in class. Keith grabbed the teacher, lifted him off the floor, and warned him never to touch Malinda again. He was made to apologize to the teacher

and leave the school, but his stepfather refused to punish him. She was only eight at the time, while he was twelve, but a bond was established, and as teenagers they became inseparable, often going for long rides in the mountains and watching the eagles circling the peaks.

It could have been any other boy–girl romance, except that the Pritchards and the Blalocks had been feuding for 150 years over all kinds of things: land rights, politics, real and imagined insults, and other reasons that no one could quite remember. It caused a stir when Keith announced he wanted to marry Malinda, but they were clearly deeply in love, so both sides agreed to call a truce— for the wedding day at least.

At the age of twenty-three, standing six feet two inches tall and weighing 220 pounds, Keith was already a formidable figure in the mountain community. No man could beat him in a fist fight, added to which he had a sharp native intelligence and political cunning. "Men either liked him or hated him, but they all noticed him," Malinda said. She was an attractive, dark-haired girl of five foot four inches tall, and her family were better off than most; several other men had tried to woo her, though as Keith saw her as his girl, they lived to regret it. One persistent suitor, John Green, had his nose, jaw, and several ribs broken by Keith in a fistfight; such outstanding evidence of passion would no doubt have impressed Malinda.

BACKGROUND
Grandfather Mountain, where Keith and Malinda courted, built their first home, and hid out from their pursuers during the war years.

On their wedding day in April 1861, Keith wore a white linen shirt and his best suit, while Malinda wore an ivory bodice and full-length skirt with dark blue flowers in her hair. Their families turned out to toast their happiness, while keeping wary eyes on each other. The ancient feud wasn't the only cause of dispute that day; the families were also split on the question of Secession. Keith's stepfather, Austin Coffey, was firmly pro-Union, but his three brothers (Keith's step-uncles) supported the Confederacy; Malinda felt the same way, and most of the Pritchards were eager to enlist with the Confederate Army. All the talk at the wedding was of the forthcoming conflict, but Keith remained non-committal: "I told them that if it came to a fight, I'd be in it. I just didn't say which side yet."

> "I told them that if it came to a fight, I'd be in it. I just didn't say which side yet."

Taking sides

Keith and Malinda built their own three-room pine cabin on Grandfather Mountain in the Blue Ridge Mountain range, planted some crops, and quickly settled in to married life, although they didn't slot into the traditional male–female roles of the time. Malinda could shoot better than most men, and would willingly accompany Keith on hunting trips along the mountain tracks; the couple hated being apart.

Meanwhile, their neighbors were still choosing sides in the war, and on May 20, 1861, North Carolina declared for the Confederates. Wherever Keith went, there were relatives or neighbors putting pressure on him to sign up, but he had a huge problem: he was anti-slavery and anti-Secession. If he followed his conscience, he would join the Union supporters who were fleeing across the mountains to enlist with the Union Army in Kentucky; but that would mean leaving Malinda behind among their largely Confederate neighbors, who might attempt to take revenge on her for her husband's allegiance. The couple could have gone into exile in the mountains for the duration of the war, but this would have meant a hand-to-mouth existence for an indeterminate length of time. Alternatively, he could bow to pressure and sign up for the Confederate Army, with the aim of getting out of it again as soon as he possibly could.

Keith chose the third option and, in June 1861, enlisted for twelve months with the 26th Carolina Infantry, but was given permission to delay his starting date until November so that he could harvest his crops. When he said goodbye to Malinda as he set off for training, she told him enigmatically that he would see her "sooner than he thought." He couldn't possibly have known how right she would be.

BELOW
Keith and Malinda knew every creek, cave, and gully of the terrain around Grandfather Mountain, in the Blue Ridge range.

As Keith marched with his regiment to Kinston Camp, North Carolina in November 1861, he looked down to see a short, slender soldier by his side, carrying a hunting rifle. He was astonished when he looked closely to find that it was Malinda, with her hair cut off, wearing the grey Confederate uniform. She had signed up as Sam Blalock, pretending to be Keith's younger brother. Keith must have been stunned, and perhaps concerned for his wife's safety, but delighted at the same time. Malinda explained that she had done it for love, adding that "Mountain women are plumb crazy about their menfolk."

Together they trained with Company F and learned all the drills. Malinda worked as hard as any man, digging trenches and building forts and bastions to hold cannons. She also prepared meals for the men, once they realized she was a decent cook, but no one ever suspected she

> "Mountain women are plumb crazy about their menfolk."

wasn't male—although one or two did comment on how protective Keith was of his much smaller younger brother. At night Malinda and Keith had a glug or two of corn whiskey from a bottle he'd brought along, then slept in the same tent.

But it wasn't to last. In April 1862, during a skirmish with Union troops near the Neuse River, Malinda was shot in the shoulder. Keith carried her back to the nearest field hospital for treatment, and the doctor who examined her inevitably discovered her secret. As soon as the wound healed, she was told she would be sent home; not wanting to be parted from his beloved wife, Keith hatched a plan to leave with her. Late that night, he crept out into the woods and rolled around naked in a patch of poison ivy until his entire body was covered in blisters. Mystified by the angry rash and his high temperature, doctors gave him an immediate medical discharge, and at the end of the month Keith and Malinda made their way home together, after what he described as "six months in service and three fights."

ABOVE
Malinda wasn't alone: Francis Clalin Clayton also disguised herself as a man—Jack Williams—to fight in the 4th Missouri Artillery, and was wounded at the Battles of Shiloh and Stones River.

THE UNDERGROUND RAILROAD

In the early 19th century, networks of abolitionists created routes which slaves could use to escape to Canada or to free states—a system of inconspicuous trails known as the "Underground Railroad." There were guides to help runaways at each stage, and safe houses where they could stay. Those who were part of the "Railroad" took great personal risk, because under the terms of the Confederate Fugitive Slave Act, which had been strengthened in 1850, they could be fined $1,000 or sentenced to six months' imprisonment. It's not known how many slaves escaped in this way, but estimates range from 50,000 to 100,000. During the Civil War, the term "Underground Railroad" was extended to describe routes used by escaped Union prisoners, with safe houses where they could stay with Union sympathizers. Keith and Malinda were guides on such a route through the Appalachians, and knew all the local people who could be depended on to provide a bed for the night and a helping of food from the pot.

Becoming Union scouts

For the next six months, Keith spent his time dodging Confederate conscription agents, who soon realized that, as his rash had miraculously healed, he was eligible for conscription under the new laws passed in April 1862. He was arrested once but managed to escape, then one night the home guard turned up at the Blalock home, led by some of their Confederate neighbors, Robert Green and two of the Moore boys. Keith was shot in the shoulder as he ran for the nearby woods, but he and Malinda managed to escape into the mountains, where she tended his wound, bathing it in spring water to prevent infection. They remained in hiding that summer, occasionally guiding escaped Union prisoners across to their units in Kentucky.

During the winter of 1862–63, they encountered Union officers looking for recruits for the 10th Michigan Cavalry, and agreed to enlist, Keith as scout captain and Malinda as his aide, under the

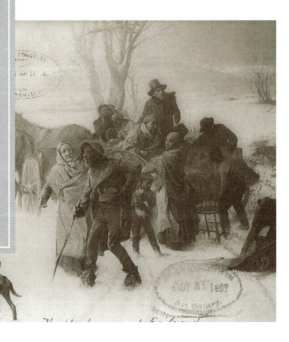

RIGHT
*African-Americans
fleeing from slavery.*

command of Colonel George W. Kirk. They were given blue Union uniforms, Colt revolvers, and the new Spencer repeating rifles, which they were amazed to find could fire twenty rounds a minute. Given that the pair were already excellent shots, these powerful weapons made them the deadliest of any guerrilla fighters in the Appalachian Mountains.

Keith and Malinda's new role was threefold: to help escaped Union prisoners get back to the Union lines; to recruit for the Union cause; and to scout on behalf of Union troops, passing back information on Confederate movements. It was work that suited them down to the ground, given their intimate knowledge of the area. However, they combined official Union business with a spot of score-settling among their neighbors, particularly Robert Green and the Moores. Adept at ambushes, they earned a reputation for robbing and plundering Confederate homesteads, stealing horses and money. Some Northern magazines, such as *Harper's Weekly*, portrayed Keith and Malinda as romantic patriots who robbed rich Confederates; but that wasn't a view shared by their victims in the

TOP
Union general Philip Kearny's division, fighting bushwhackers in the woods in Virginia.

ABOVE
The cover of Harper's Weekly *on September 5, 1863 showed guerrillas attacking a wagon train.*

SWITCHING SIDES IN THE WAR

The Blalocks were not unique in changing their allegiance during the war; it was relatively common in border territory or occupied lands, such as northern Alabama or eastern Tennessee. If a man met recruiting agents on the road and they gave him a choice (possibly at gunpoint) between imprisonment or signing up for their side, he often made the expedient decision. Officially, switching sides was counted as treason and the penalty was death, but there is evidence of hundreds of soldiers changing their allegiance and switching to either Union or Confederate armies—although fewer changed to the Confederates once it became clear they were losing. If a man chose the "wrong" side, though, he might find it difficult to return home after the war and face the wrath of his neighbors. And if he died fighting for the "wrong" side, he could be denied burial in the family plot at the local graveyard.

terrorized mountain community, who regarded them as "no better than bushwhackers"—in other words, common criminals.

Such forays, however, were fraught with hazard. During an attack on the Moores' family farm in September 1863, Malinda was injured in the forearm and shoulder. Keith managed to get her over the mountains to a Union field hospital in Knoxville, where her wounds were treated and where it was also found that she was pregnant. The child, a son she named Columbus, was born on April 8, 1864, in the home of a Knoxville woman friend, but no sooner had Malinda given birth than she was back in the mountains with Keith, leaving relatives to care for her baby. She would barely see him again until he was two years old.

Strike and counterstrike

The revenge shootings continued, with Confederate neighbors targeting Blalock relatives since they couldn't catch Keith and Malinda: Malinda's cousin, Thomas Pritchard, and Keith's stepfather, Austin Coffey, were killed, and the list of people on whom the Blalocks were determined to avenge themselves grew longer. When asked how such murders could be part of the war effort, Keith replied, "We all tried to do to them before they did to us." He never lied about a murder, and always took credit for the men he killed. Their enemies claimed that Malinda was as ruthless as him, but Keith defended her by saying that she "never shot an unarmed man."

Between 1863 and 1865, Keith was responsible for a number of shootings unrelated to the war: the murder of Robert Green, who with the Moores had brought the home guard to Keith's house; the killing of his Confederate step-uncle, William Coffey; the shooting and crippling of Jesse Moore; the burning down of the house of McCaleb Coffey, another step-uncle; and "putting a bullet in" Calvin Green. After the war was over, he ambushed and killed

John Boyd, whom he considered responsible for his stepfather's murder; he later stood trial for this crime but escaped punishment, successfully using an argument of self-defence.

> "We all tried to do to them before they did to us."

It didn't always go the Blalocks' way, though; when he attacked Lott Green's house, Keith sustained a serious injury to his forearm that would leave it twisted and largely useless for the rest of his life. Then during a second attack on the Moores' home, he was shot in the eye. The ball lodged inside his skull, and the eye was lost completely, though he somehow survived, nursed by Malinda, who gave him shots of corn whiskey for the pain. Thereafter he wore a patch over the empty socket, but suffered severe recurrent headaches for the rest of his life.

Following Robert E. Lee's surrender in April 1865, Malinda went back to collect her son Columbus from her relatives in east Tennessee. Columbus later said that she "used to tell me that she met me at two . . . I was too young to think anything of it." She grew her hair, and when Keith saw her again he said she once more looked like "the girl he had courted and married."

BELOW
Skirmishes were common throughout the Civil War as scouting parties came upon their opposite numbers.

Keith was medically discharged from the Union Army and successfully applied for a wounded veterans' pension, much to the disgust of the neighbors he had terrorized. They complained to the authorities and tried several times to get it rescinded, without success. Keith and Malinda became farmers, and had four sons altogether, bringing them up in the same mountain ways that they themselves had learned as children. Keith even had an unsuccessful stint in local politics.

When Malinda died in her sleep in 1903, aged sixty-one, Keith was devastated. Most days he walked several miles to visit her grave. But he also took up a new hobby after she was gone, whizzing around mountain tracks on a railroad handcar he had bought, which he operated by pumping a handle up and down. On the morning of April 11, 1913, his handcar flew off the tracks on a notorious bend, and he died in the fall. He was buried alongside Malinda, the woman he had been utterly devoted to since protecting her from a teacher's switch when she was eight.

BELOW
In 1913, Keith was laid to rest alongside Malinda in Montezuma Cemetery, Avery County, North Carolina.

In the end, only death could separate them.

It's an unconventional love story, but there was never any doubt about the depth of their love. In the end, only death could separate them.

ABOVE
Each cavalryman was responsible for the care of his own horse.

BELOW
The Confederate Army had entire cavalry units, while at first the Union Army just used horsemen as scouts and pickets. This changed during the course of the war as the strategic advantages of being on horseback were recognized.

HORSES IN THE WAR

Horses were vital to both sides during the war: for cavalry units, transporting goods in wagons, hauling ambulance carts and cannons; for letting scouts check on enemy positions and carry messages from camp to camp; and for generals to ride in battle. Southerners had the advantage because horse racing was a popular sport and they were more practiced riders, used to crossing rough terrain, whereas in the North there were more roads and wheeled conveyances. Horse theft was commonplace in border lands, and the Blalocks were past masters at it. It was a tough war for horses and mules, though, with at least a million dying. More perished of disease and exhaustion than from their wounds, but still the big battles took their toll, with around 1,500 horses killed at Gettysburg alone.

Absolom A. Harrison
(May 3, 1831–May 13, 1914)

Susan Elizabeth Allstun
(February 2, 1836–December 31, 1920)

MARRIED: *May 18, 1854*

ARMY: *Union*

RANK & DIVISION: *Quartermaster sergeant, 4ᵗʰ Regiment Kentucky Cavalry Volunteers*

BATTLES FOUGHT: *None, but was with his company when it fought at Lebanon and Murfreesboro*

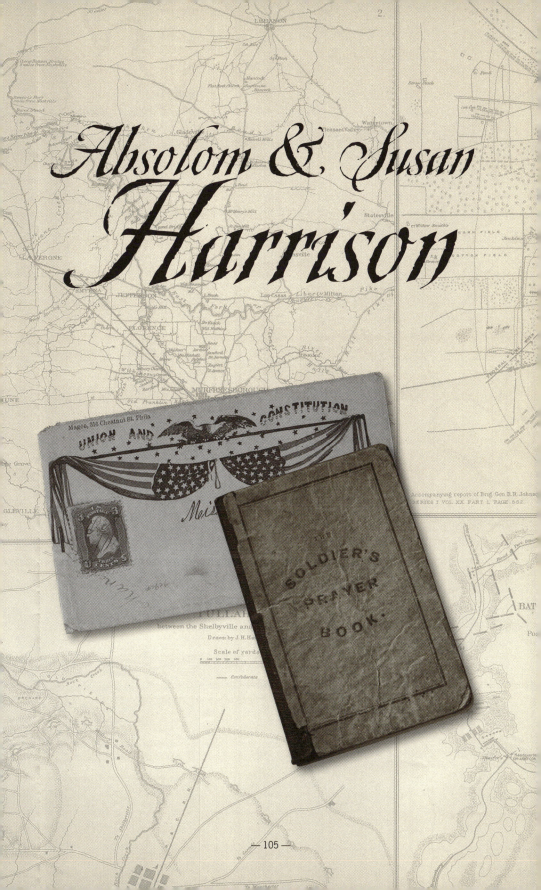

Absolom & Susan
Harrison

Absolom Harrison, a distant cousin of Abraham Lincoln, was swept up in a Union recruitment drive in October 1861, and didn't write to tell his wife he had enlisted until almost two months later. Stuck at home with three children to care for and another on the way, she can't have welcomed the news.

Abraham Lincoln was a Kentucky man, born in Hodgenville into a poor backwoods family, but from the start he was driven to better himself. He worked as a manual laborer, storekeeper, postmaster, and militia captain, all the while reading every book he could lay his hands on, before entering politics at the age of twenty-three while simultaneously studying to become a lawyer. In 1861, he attained the height of his ambition when he became his country's 16th president.

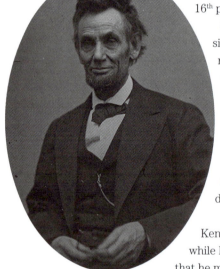

Susan Allstun's grandmother was Lincoln's sister, making Susan a first cousin once removed of the president, and by all accounts she was a similarly driven character. She came from a farming family, but learned to read and write fluently in an era when few farmers' daughters were educated. Her husband-to-be, Absolom Harrison, a third cousin once removed of Lincoln, also seems to have shared his determination to improve himself.

Absolom's parents moved to Hardin County, Kentucky, in the 1840s, and it may have been while he was in Elizabethtown buying supplies that he met Susan, the eldest of nine children, who at the time was responsible for raising five of her siblings. She was a clever woman, quite unusual for her era and her station in life, and it seems she became the driving force in their relationship. Absolom was bowled over by her and keen to share her vision of a prosperous future. They married in May 1854 and a daughter was born in June 1855, the first of thirteen children they would have together.

ABOVE
Abraham Lincoln only grew a beard after an eleven-year-old girl wrote to him on the eve of the 1860 election saying he should grow whiskers because his face was too thin.

Forced to take sides

Much-loved Kentucky politician Henry Clay had three times
negotiated compromise treaties between the Northern and
Southern states, regarding issues such as the establishment
of state boundaries and the treatment of slaves. Many felt in
retrospect that with his death in 1852 went the only chance
of averting war nine years later. As it was, in April 1861 Fort
Sumter in South Carolina was attacked by Confederate troops
and hostilities commenced.

Kentucky was in an unenviable position. Its northern border
along the Ohio River was seen by many as a symbolic frontier
between the slave-owning South and the free North. Militarily,
it would have been easier for the Confederates to defend than
other borders further south, making it desirable territory for
both sides. Kentucky was tied economically to the North, but
surrounded by Confederate neighbors. Kentuckians had voted
for Lincoln in the 1860 election, and the people remained divided.
In some cases there were differing allegiances within the same
family—famously, in the case of Kentucky Senator John Crittenden's
two sons, one of whom became a Confederate general and the
other a Union one.

At first, Kentucky declared itself neutral, but such neutrality
could not last, with both armies traveling from town to town
trying to drum up volunteers. The tipping point came when the

ABOVE
*Patriotic fever: Union
soldiers on their way
to war, accompanied
by a marching band.*

Confederate Army invaded southern Kentucky in September 1861, prompting the state as a whole to declare for the Union, though two-fifths of Kentuckians would still sign up to fight for the Confederates.

On October 20, 1861, Absolom Harrison and his brother Jo were mustered into the Union Army during a recruitment drive. It isn't clear whether they chose this side because of their family connection with Lincoln or in a spirit of patriotic fervor after the Confederate invasion, but whatever the reason they were marched off to Camp Anderson to begin training with the 4th Kentucky Cavalry. Absolom wrote on December 12, telling Susan, "I have enlisted and been sworn in," while adding that they hadn't yet received horses or uniforms. He promised that as soon as they were paid he would either send money to her or, preferably, bring it himself—an over-optimistic claim, as it would be another ten months before he saw his family again.

Susan was stuck at home on their farm near Elizabethtown with three children under the age of seven and another one on the way. Their baby son Robert had died in June that year at the age of just three months, which would have made it a difficult

OPPOSITE
The Union cavalry-man's uniform with blue kepi and a caped overcoat.

BELOW
The Louisville & Nashville Railroad—here crossing a bridge over the Mississippi in Louisville—was crucial for getting supplies to troops on the Western front.

time for any family. She must surely have been
furious with Absolom for leaving her, despite his
promise that he would send money soon, and his
closing greeting, "remaining your affectionate
husband until death." Could that be why
he complains so frequently in his
letters that he has hardly received
any from her? Was she giving him
the silent treatment?

> *"I have enlisted and been sworn in."*

Safer at the front than at home

During that winter of 1861–62,
Absolom wrote to Susan
complaining of the rigors of army
life. His daily routine was: roll
call at 6 a.m., horses to be fed and
groomed, breakfast, then drill on
foot until lunchtime. After lunch
they had a drill on horseback

until 4 p.m., then the horses had to be fed and groomed before they collected wood for the night. He said there wasn't enough food to go around, that they slept on blankets laid on waterlogged ground, and that although they hadn't yet confronted the enemy directly there were frequent skirmishes that meant he had to help bury, on average, four fellow soldiers a day. "If I live to get out of this I will never be caught soldiering again, that is certain," he wrote.

In fact, Susan and his children were possibly more in danger than he was, as friends and neighbors turned on each other in Hardin County. There were ambushes, firefights, families were harassed, menfolk were murdered, and homes set ablaze in what became known as the "Blackberry Patch War." Susan wrote to Absolom pleading with him to let her move the family to safety, but he urged her to stay put. "I want you to stay where you are at and be as content as you can," he wrote, before blithely assuring her that God (or Providence) would see them through all difficulties.

In April, Susan gave birth to a daughter, her fifth child, and still she kept insisting to him that she wanted to move the family out of harm's way. In August 1862, he wrote, "You don't know how it would grieve me to think you would go any place else after you had promised me to stay where you was." Was he afraid that it would be hard to find her during wartime if she moved? Or did he want her to stay at home in order to guard their property? Her letters haven't survived, but she does appear to have obeyed—although not without frequent complaint.

> "If I live to get out of this I will never be caught soldiering again, that is certain."

The Confederates were driven out of most of Kentucky, and Absolom's brigade marched south to Nashville, where he was made quartermaster sergeant in charge of supplies. It meant that he remained in camp looking after the stores and missed his company's engagement at Lebanon, Tennessee, that May when they beat back a raiding force led by General John Hunt Morgan (whom Absolom called "a notorious Ky. [Kentucky] Robber"). When the company fought at Murfreesboro in July, Absolom was off fetching supplies and found himself on the wrong side of a bridge that had been destroyed; he had to hitch a ride with another company in order to get back to camp.

He did not escape his war service scot-free, though, as in August he fell ill with malaria, and the following month was given a medical discharge to come home and recuperate. His brother Jo was also discharged, but by that time he was too weak to travel and died of pneumonia on September 14 in an army hospital in Nashville.

An itinerant lifestyle

Absolom arrived home to meet his new baby daughter and to mourn his brother. He was pleased that conscription laws were passed in October, forcing white men aged from eighteen to forty-five to register for service. He hoped they would draft some of the "Secesh [Secession] boys" who were causing so much trouble in Kentucky and force them to fight fairly and squarely instead of using guerrilla tactics against their neighbors. He was also pleased when a bill

KENTUCKY RAIDERS

General John Hunt Morgan was a Kentucky boy and knew the state like the back of his hand. During his daredevil raids in July 1862, December 1862, and July 1863, he knew how to inflict maximum damage on Union troops and supply lines. In the last of these, known as Morgan's raid, he got all the way to the Ohio River and crossed into southern Indiana before being forced to surrender. He was jailed in Ohio Penitentiary but in November tunneled his way out. Major General Nathan Bedford Forrest led another raid into Kentucky in 1864, and smaller groups of guerrilla fighters continued to cause havoc wherever they could. In an attempt to clamp down on guerrilla activity, military rule was imposed that summer under Major General Stephen Burbridge. He soon became known as "the Butcher of Kentucky" because of his edict that whenever a Union officer was killed anywhere in the state, four guerrillas would be taken at random from prison and executed.

LEFT
John Hunt Morgan was a law unto himself, prone to disobeying orders from his superior officers.

THE ALL-IMPORTANT RAILROADS

In January 1862, Lincoln passed an act that gave the War Department full authority over the rail network, and hired engineers to lay more track where it was needed. That meant Union generals could use the railroad to transport supplies of food, weapons, and uniforms to the men, giving them a huge strategic advantage. By the end of the war, they had built 4,000 extra miles of track, while the South had only built an extra 400 miles. Destroying railway bridges was a popular Confederate tactic, but Union engineers proved able to get them up and functioning again in record time. The Louisville and Nashville (L & N) railroad that ran through Elizabethtown was frequently targeted.

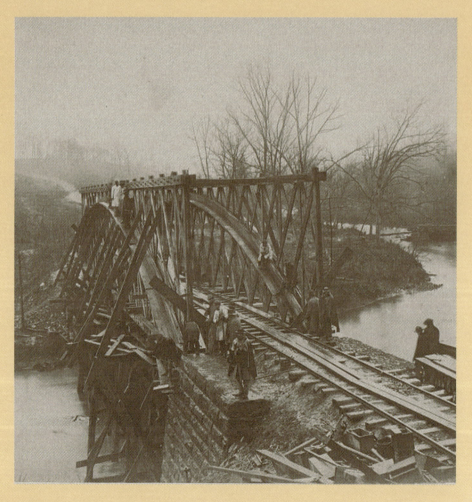

ABOVE
*Union engineers building a new bridge over Bull Run, a
stream where two major Civil War battles were fought.*

was passed allowing rebels' property to be confiscated. But it was not long before he learned that these measures were far from sufficient to make Hardin County a safe place to raise a family.

Throughout the second half of 1862, the Confederate Army kept trying to retake Kentucky, but President Lincoln was determined not to let them: "To lose Kentucky is nearly the same as to lose the whole game," he wrote to an Illinois senator. Confederates Major General Edmund Kirby Smith and General

> *"To lose Kentucky is nearly the same as to lose the whole game."*

Braxton Bragg moved into the state in August and began battling their way north, hoping to be welcomed as liberators, but found there was less enthusiasm than they had anticipated from the war-weary inhabitants. By late October they had been driven out, though the state remained a battleground.

Absolom's malaria recurred in November 1862, leaving him bedridden for several weeks. He felt particularly helpless in December when John Hunt Morgan launched the so-called "Christmas raid" into Kentucky with the aim of disrupting Union supply lines on the Louisville and Nashville railroad. Morgan moved north, shelling Elizabethtown and burning bridges just 10 miles away from the Harrisons' homestead. He managed to capture some 1,886 Union officers and destroy two million dollars' worth of Union property, including huge stretches of the railroad. Finally, this was enough to persuade Absolom that he had to get his family out of the state. No doubt Susan was mightily relieved.

BELOW
The railway bridge over the Rappahannock River in eastern Virginia was burned in October 1863, just before the Battle of Rappahannock Station.

A NATION MOURNS

At 10 p.m. on April 14, 1865, John Wilkes Booth crept into the box at Ford's Theatre in Washington D.C., where the president was watching a comedy entitled *Our American Cousin*. Shouting *"Sic semper tyrannis"* ("Thus always to tyrants"), Booth fired a single shot through Lincoln's skull, just above the left ear. The president was carried to a boarding house across the street, but never regained consciousness. Crowds gathered outside and, according to Secretary of the Navy Gideon Welles, "intense grief was on every countenance . . . The colored people especially—and there were at this time more of them, perhaps, than of whites— were overwhelmed with grief." Lincoln died at 7:22 a.m. the next morning. It was the first time a U.S. president had been assassinated, an event that united most Americans in shock and grief.

As soon as the railroad was functioning again, in March 1863, the Harrisons moved north to Lebanon, Indiana, along with Absolom's father and several other family members. They rented some land and Absolom earned a living as a tenant farmer. They were to move five times over the next twelve years, during which period he tried various occupations, including teaching (he gained a first-class teaching certificate) and running general stores. Susan gave birth to their thirteenth child, a son, in 1879, by which time she was forty-three years old and must have been worn out! That same year, Absolom applied for a war pension, in his application describing the still-frequent attacks of malaria that left him bedridden for up to three months at a time.

The final push

Despite Absolom's ill health, the couple remained determined to better themselves. In 1880, they moved back to Kentucky, and the following year were among a party roughly twenty-strong that moved to Sikeston, Missouri, a frontier town with vast swamps where land could be bought very cheaply. For those who had the energy and know-how to drain it, this proved to be fertile farming country that made their fortunes. Several of the party succumbed to swamp fever, but for the Harrisons it was a route to the prosperity they had long sought.

By 1900, they had a substantial farm and a large general store, and Absolom was a justice of the peace, responsible for performing local marriages. Their children married and produced grandchildren, and at last Absolom and Susan could sit back and reap the rewards of their years of struggle.

It was a marriage that had been through some very tough patches. You only have to look at his final war letter to her to understand that: "I have not received a letter from you . . . It cannot be that you have forgotten me as soon as I was out of sight . . . The other boys here are getting letters all the time from the same neighborhood. . . If you have not wrote yet I want you to write and tell me the reason."

She might have been furious with him but Susan didn't ever leave him. She saved all his letters, even if she didn't always reply to them. She waited for him to come back from the war, nursed him through his bouts of malaria, bore him thirteen children, and, at an age when many would have sat back and lived off a war pension, the two of them took on the tough challenge of turning swamp land into a thriving farm. Finally, they became the prosperous, respectable people they had strived to be all along. Their journey was tougher than most, but they had those Lincoln genes giving them the grit necessary to succeed.

OPPOSITE
The room in which President Lincoln died was small and overcrowded. At six feet four inches, he was too long for the bed in which he lay.

Their journey was tougher than most, but they had those Lincoln genes giving them the grit necessary to succeed.

Sullivan Ballou
(March 28, 1829–July 21, 1861)

MARRIED: *October 15, 1855*

ARMY: *Union*

RANK & DIVISION: *Major in 2nd Rhode Island Volunteers*

BATTLES FOUGHT: *First Bull Run*

Sarah Hart Shumway
(February 26, 1837–April 19, 1917)

Sullivan & Sarah Ballou

S. Ballou

Sullivan Ballou was raised by a single mother and couldn't bear the thought that his wife Sarah would have to raise their two sons on her own. Yet when he wrote to her on the evening of July 14, 1861, a week before he would march into the first major battle of the Civil War, he anticipated exactly that eventuality.

ABOVE
When war began, Sullivan Ballou was a thirty-two-year-old husband and father of two young boys, with a thriving law practice and political ambitions.

Sullivan Ballou and Sarah Shumway grew up just 30 miles apart, at opposite ends of the Blackstone River—his family in Smithfield, Rhode Island, hers in Worcester, Massachusetts. Sullivan's family were distinguished folk, of Huguenot origin, linked by blood to President Fillmore. However, Sullivan's father died when he was just four years old, leaving his mother Emeline to bring him up on her own, along with his sisters Janette and Hannah. Money was tight, but the extended family helped out, and his mother managed to send Sullivan to Phillips Academy in Andover, then to Brown University in Providence, before he left to study law in Ballston, New York. He was admitted to the Rhode Island Bar in 1853, but from the start was ambitious to be more than just a lawyer. Politics was in his veins, and when he began courting Sarah Shumway, a doctor's daughter, he told her of his plans.

Sarah was an intelligent young woman with progressive ideas, so theirs was a meeting of both hearts and minds, such that it soon became the "unbounded love" of which Sullivan would later write to her on the eve of war. They were married in 1855, in Poughkeepsie, New York, where her family then resided. Their first son, Edgar, was born the following year and the second, William, in 1859, yet still romance flourished and he wrote her love letters whenever they were apart: "how foolish, a man of my age. . . should still be <u>really</u> in <u>love</u> with his wife [and] disconsolate without her." Sullivan and Sarah set up home in Woonsocket, Rhode Island, a town where the main industry was the textile mills powered by the waters of the Blackstone River. Sullivan had family connections there, including a cousin, Latimer Ballou, a prominent banker. Woonsocket was also close enough that he could travel to the Providence law firm in which he and his friend Charles F. Brownell were partners.

All the while, Sullivan was taking his first steps towards a career in politics. He served as a clerk of the Rhode Island House of Representatives from 1853 to 1857, became a member of the House in 1857, and was chosen as speaker by unanimous vote in the same year. Like many Northerners, he was disillusioned by the Whig and Democrat parties and, in the late 1850s, joined the newly formed Republican Party, which was firmly anti-slavery while being in favor of modernization and expansion of industry, banking, and railroads, and "free soil"—the grant of land to farmers in the West. When Abraham Lincoln was chosen as Republican presidential candidate, Sullivan threw himself wholeheartedly into the campaign. He made the acquaintance of William Sprague—a wealthy mill owner who in 1860 became governor of Rhode Island—and decided to cultivate the contact, which he thought could be advantageous in the future. Sarah was completely behind him and excited about his plans to change the world for the better through his political work.

Sullivan had everything to live for: a loving wife and two young sons at home, a good job, and a burgeoning political career. But when Fort Sumter fell to Confederate troops, the whole picture changed.

EXPERIENCE NOT ESSENTIAL

Before conscription was introduced in late 1862, companies were raised by local leaders using their personal influence and even their own money. The men elected their own officers, and military experience was not necessarily one of the foremost criteria: wealth, social status, and popularity also played a part. Many officers, while being patriotic and committed, had never handled a rifle before, never mind led men into battle. William Sprague, who was only twenty-nine when he became Rhode Island state governor in 1860, was typical of these enthusiasts. He believed the Civil War would last only 48 hours, and had no hesitation in raising volunteer regiments and accompanying them to the Battle of First Bull Run. But when it became apparent the war would last much longer, he turned down an offer to become brigadier general of volunteers, deciding that politics was safer. Exam boards were introduced to weed out incompetent generals and, by May 1862, 310 officers had been expelled from the Union Army.

LEFT *Governor William Sprague.*

"All green alike"

Sullivan had no military experience, but as a matter of conscience felt he must volunteer as soon as war began. He explained his reasoning to Sarah and, although she must have been terrified of what the future could hold, she knew he was a man of good conscience and so supported his decision. He later reiterated his reasons in a letter, saying, "I know how strongly American Civilization now leans upon the triumph of the Government," and acknowledging his debt to those who went through "the blood and suffering of the Revolution." Besides, like most people in the North, he thought the conflict would be short. When Abraham Lincoln called for volunteers, Governor William Sprague formed the 1st Rhode Island Volunteers with men who had enlisted for three months; it was followed by the 2nd, with three-year enlistment, in which Sprague offered Sullivan a position as major. He accepted, though with a heavy heart, writing to his cousin Latimer, "The bare thought of leaving my wife and boys is full of intense pain."

> "*The bare thought of leaving my wife and boys is full of intense pain.*"

The 2nd Rhode Island regiment received just a month of training in Providence before being kitted out with their Union uniforms—blue flannel shirts, gray pants, and forage caps—so that on June 19, 1861, they paraded out of town, watched by huge crowds of cheering townspeople. Sullivan marched at the front, along with their commander, Colonel John Slocum. Sarah was probably there, too, with the couple's young sons, waving and trying to suppress her tears. The men boarded the steamship *State of Maine*, which took them to Port Elizabeth, New Jersey, and from there it was on to Washington by train.

ABOVE
A soldier from the 2nd Rhode Island Volunteers, Sullivan's regiment, poses for a studio photograph.

The 2nd Rhode Island regiment was based at Camp Clark, Washington, D.C. The day after their arrival Sullivan wrote to Sarah, "We are encamped in paradise . . . It is an oak grove—the trees all tall and large and the ground free of shrubs." His horse Jennie was tied up just behind his tent. Sarah's letters have not survived, but she wrote to him every Sunday with news of their

ABOVE
*The heartfelt letter Sullivan
left in his trunk, to be forwarded
to Sarah if he fell in battle.*

RIGHT
*The 1st Rhode Island Volunteers
at Camp Sprague near
Washington, D.C.*

two boys and life in their hometown. He missed them terribly: "I never knew the longing of a father for his children before," he wrote. Sullivan and Captain Smith, a friend from Woonsocket, began to make plans for their wives to visit them at the camp. Meanwhile, on June 24, the regiment marched to the White House and were reviewed by Sullivan's idol, Abraham Lincoln himself, before the president and his wife visited them at Camp Clark on July 2.

Confederate troops were based just 30 miles to the south of Washington, and Lincoln planned a preemptive strike, which he hoped would be quick and decisive. Union General Irvin McDowell pleaded for more time to train his recruits, but Lincoln responded, "You are green and they are green also. You are all green alike." He hoped for a swift end to the war, and felt sure that their superior numbers—35,000 to just 18,000 Confederate troops in the area—would prevail. It was not to be so.

The Battle of First Bull Run

The men in Camp Clark knew that battle was imminent and must have felt very apprehensive and emotional as they waited for marching orders. During the day of July 14, 1861, Sullivan wrote a letter to Sarah telling her it was possible that they would move on to Virginia soon but that he did not "apprehend fighting on a large scale." However, that evening he wrote another letter, one he didn't post but left behind in his trunk, intending that it would be forwarded to her in the event of his death. In it, he reiterated the reasons why he felt he had to fight but also wrote of his deep love for her, saying, "the memories of all the blissful moments I have spent with you, come creeping over me." He described how hard it was to contemplate leaving her if things did not go well for him, but wrote that, if it should be so, "when my last breath escapes me on the battlefield, it will whisper your name."

> " . . . when my last breath escapes me on the battlefield, it will whisper your name."

He asked Sarah's forgiveness for all his faults and the times when he was thoughtless and caused her pain: "How gladly I would . . . struggle with all the misfortunes of the world to shield you and my children from harm." He was sadly aware that William was too young to remember him, and that Edgar would have but "the dimmest memories," but told of his "unlimited confidence in her maternal care," saying he knew she would raise them to "honorable manhood." He asked her, "Sarah, do not mourn me dead; think I am gone and wait for thee, for we shall meet again." It was a poignant, thoughtful letter to the love of his life, bidding her an early farewell. It must have broken his heart to write it.

On the morning of July 17, Sullivan's regiment marched across the Potomac into Virginia, along with the 1st Rhode Island, the 2nd New Hampshire Volunteers, and the 71st New York Militia—all commanded by Colonel Ambrose Burnside. They expected a battle at Fairfax Court House, but as Ballou wrote to Sarah that day, "the enemy departed in great haste, leaving almost everything" —including the Confederate flag, retrieved from the top of the court house. The retreat made Union troops more confident of victory, as did the crowds who came to cheer them every step of the way as they marched through Centreville and on towards Manassas, an important railroad junction.

At 2 a.m. on July 21, they assembled for battle. Colonel Slocum and Sullivan Ballou led their men from the front as they forded

BELOW
When Colonel Burnside's men attacked the Confederate batteries in the Battle of First Bull Run, they didn't know that spies had reported their battle plans to the enemy.

ARMY RATIONS

Official U.S. Army daily rations were 12 oz. of bacon or pork, or 1 lb. 4 oz. of fresh or salt beef, and 1 lb. 6 oz. of soft bread or flour, 1 lb. of hard bread (hard tack) or 1 lb. 4 oz. of cornmeal. They were also issued with beans or peas, rice or hominy, coffee, tea, sugar, vinegar, candles, soap, and molasses. Marching rations were less generous, with just 1 lb. of hard bread, ¾ lb. of salt pork or 1¼ lb. of fresh meat per man per day, plus sugar, coffee, and salt. Fresh vegetables were sometimes available, though not always. Soon after his arrival at Camp Clark, Sullivan wrote to Sarah, "I would give one hundred dollars if I could get a good meal." In 1861, Confederate rations were the same as those given to the Union Army, but from spring 1862 they were reduced, and soldiers often went hungry due to difficulties in distribution. After the surrender at Appomattox Court House which ended the war, the Confederate Army was literally starving, and Union general Ulysses S. Grant's offer of rations was gratefully received.

RIGHT
Prisoners of war were at the back of the line when rations were distributed.

Bull Run stream and ran straight into enemy fire. Colonel Slocum was shot in the head as he straddled a fence to wave on the men, and was carried off on a stretcher. Sullivan rallied the men and led the advance up Matthews Hill, but, soon after, he was struck by a cannonball that killed his horse and pulverized his right leg. Both men were taken to a field hospital in nearby Sudley Church, where Sullivan's leg was amputated.

Back on the battlefield the fighting raged on. So confident of victory was the Union side that civilians, including congressmen and their wives, came out to watch, some even bringing a picnic. They were in for a shock. The Union brigades prevailed at first, but the Confederates had not only received advance warning of their tactics and were able to counterattack; they also had reinforcements on the way, including General Stonewall Jackson's unit. The fighting continued into the 22nd, in driving rain, and eventually the Union Army was forced to retreat across Long Bridge into Washington, hindered by the spectators who got in their way.

As Union troops fell back, Confederates advanced towards Sudley Church so quickly that there was no time to move the wounded men being treated there; Colonel Slocum and Sullivan

Ballou soon found themselves in enemy hands. Slocum died of his injuries on the 23rd, while Sullivan lay, feverish and alone, for another five days, until on July 28 he succumbed to infection.

Altogether, 2,896 Union soldiers were killed or wounded, or went missing, in that first battle of the war, among them 114 men of the 1,000-strong 2nd Rhode Island Volunteers. A witness told President Lincoln that it was really a Union victory, to which the President's reply was scathing: "So it's your notion that we whipped the rebels, and then ran away from them?" In the South, many celebrated, believing they had won the war.

Back at camp, Ballou's trunk, containing the extraordinary farewell letter he had written two weeks before his death, was located and returned to Sarah by Governor Sprague. It must have brought her some small comfort, reading his beautiful letter— almost like hearing his voice from beyond the grave.

Honorable manhood

Eight months after the Battle of First Bull Run, when Governor Sprague accompanied the Union troops once again advancing on Manassas Junction, this time unopposed, his first thought was to find and recover the bodies of Colonel Slocum and Sullivan Ballou. A local woman told him that Slocum's grave had been dug up by Confederates and his corpse beheaded while the remainder was

---

"If there be a soft breeze upon your cheek, it shall be . . . my spirit passing by."

---

burned. She showed them the spot, where they did indeed find a mixture of ashes and bones, and nearby a white shirt belonging to Sullivan. It seems that some Confederate soldiers mistook him for the colonel and took revenge on him for losses their regiment had suffered during the battle. Sprague ordered that the remains be collected and placed in a coffin. On March 31, 1862, Colonel Slocum and Sullivan Ballou were both given formal funerals in Providence. Local businesses closed in their honor, flags were lowered to half-mast, bells tolled, and cannons were fired, before the two were buried in Swan Point Cemetery.

A widow at the age of twenty-four, Sarah must have felt proud as she watched the ceremony. Yet despite all the plaudits she would surely much rather have had her husband back home safe with her and their boys. It must have seemed desperately unfair that her husband was among the very first Union casualties. She didn't know then that the war would last four years and see the deaths of around 625,000 men.

Sarah was awarded a government pension of $25 a month plus $2 a month for each child, but this would never make up for losing the love of her life and the father who would never see their sons grow up to "honorable manhood." She raised them herself, supplementing her income by teaching piano, and from 1875 to 1899 acting as secretary of the Providence School Committee.

Sarah never remarried, perhaps because no one could have lived up to her romantic, dashing first husband. Besides, she believed he was still with her in spirit, as he wrote, "If there be a soft breeze upon your cheek, it shall be my breath, as the cool air fans your throbbing temple, it shall be my spirit passing by."

When she died in 1917, she left a request that words from Sullivan's letter should be carved on her gravestone: "Come to me and lead thither my children." Many copies of the letter were made, but no one knows for sure what happened to the original. It seems likely that Sarah took it with her to the grave.

CIVIL WAR FLAGS

Just before the Civil War began, the United States national flag had seven red stripes and thirty-three stars, a number that remained unchanged when Southern states seceded from the Union, because Secession was deemed illegal in the North. In the South, a Confederate flag called the "Stars and Bars" was produced in March 1861, with seven stars and three bars, and this was altered to add more stars as further states seceded. However, it was felt the design was too close to that of the Stars and Stripes, and could thus be mistaken for it. So a new design was created showing thirteen stars running along a blue cross on a red background; this became the Confederate battle flag. Each regiment also had its own flag, often based on state insignia, which the men would follow in battle. It was a point of honor to keep the flag flying, to prevent its capture at all costs. If the man carrying the flag fell, someone else would step in to retrieve it.

TOP
A Union soldier carrying "Old Glory," the Union flag. Flagbearers would defend the flag at all costs.

ABOVE
The Union flag on a Civil War envelope.

RIGHT
The Confederate "Stars and Bars," with eleven stars representing the eleven states that had seceded from the Union.

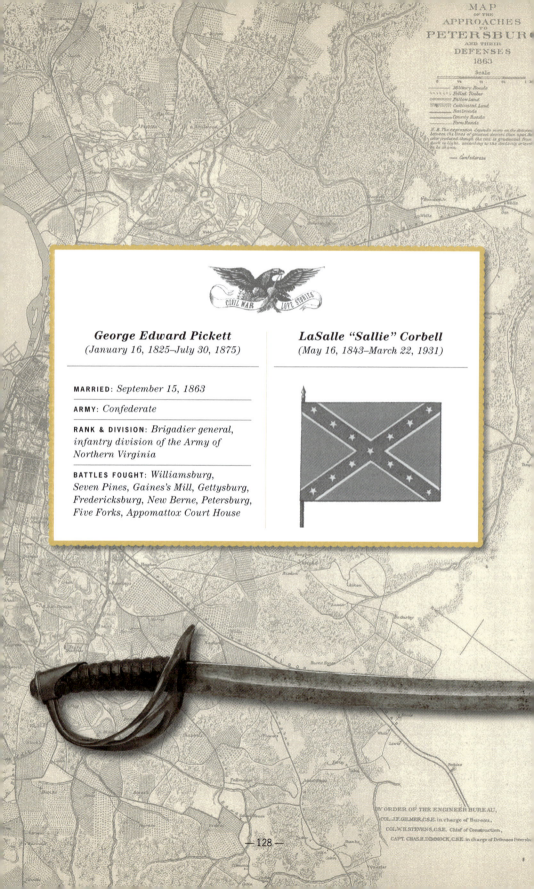

George Edward Pickett
(January 16, 1825–July 30, 1875)

MARRIED: *September 15, 1863*

ARMY: *Confederate*

RANK & DIVISION: *Brigadier general, infantry division of the Army of Northern Virginia*

BATTLES FOUGHT: *Williamsburg, Seven Pines, Gaines's Mill, Gettysburg, Fredericksburg, New Berne, Petersburg, Five Forks, Appomattox Court House*

LaSalle "Sallie" Corbell
(May 16, 1843–March 22, 1931)

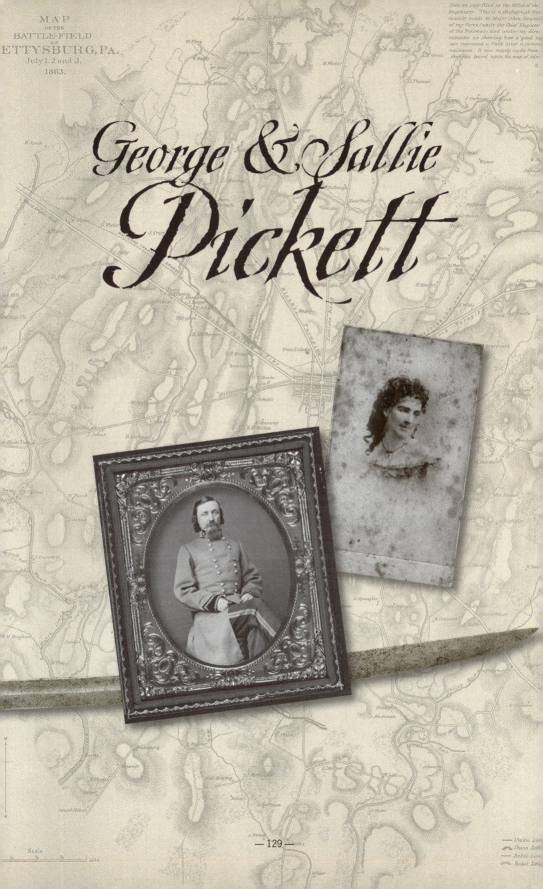

George & Sallie Pickett

After her husband's death, Sallie did her best to sanctify his memory by publishing his wartime letters to her, but it has since been suggested that she falsified some. Today history records him as the man who lost half his division at Gettysburg during what became known as Pickett's Charge.

George Pickett looked quite the dandy, with a curled mustache and long hair styled in highly perfumed ringlets. He was particular about his clothing, choosing shirts of fine white linen with ruffles at the sleeves and neck. At West Point Military Academy, his refusal to wear the regulation stiff collars earned him several demerits, and his fondness for practical jokes brought many more, but he didn't appear to care. He was happy to come bottom of his class, having done precisely enough to graduate and no more.

George served in the Mexican–American War and in January 1851, at the age of twenty-six, he married the first Sally in his life—Sally Harrison Minge, the great-great-granddaughter of President Harrison. But the marriage was tragically short-lived, as Sally died in childbirth that November, along with the child.

The second Sallie claims she met her future husband shortly after his first wife's death, when he was still in mourning. She was just nine years old and visiting a friend of her grandmother's at Old Point Comfort on the Virginia coast when she came upon him lying in the garden, reading. He told her he had lost someone very dear to him and, she recalls, "without so much as a by-your-leave, I promised to take the place of his dear one and to comfort him in his loss," upon which they became "engaged." It's a romantic story but one that is challenged by critics, as his letters show that even had they met back then, they certainly could not have become properly engaged: George never met her father, so couldn't have asked for her hand. It would be another eleven years before Sallie would get the man she called 'my Soldier' to the altar—during which time he fell passionately in love with, and married, another.

"...I promised to take the place of his dear one and to comfort him in his loss."

ABOVE
George Pickett came last in his class at West Point, where his contemporaries included future Civil War luminaries such as George B. McLellan, Thomas Jackson, and A.P. Hill.

Morning Mist

George Pickett's next posting was to Bellingham in Washington state, near the Canadian border, to supervise the construction of a fort, and to protect local Native Americans from other tribes who periodically attacked from the North. While on a visit to Semiahmoo Bay, he met and fell for a girl from the Haida tribe called Sâkis Tiigang, a name which means "Morning Mist." In those days, there were many instances of white men trapping Native Americans into sham marriages, then disappearing over the horizon, leaving behind a mixed-race child. However, George Pickett insisted that if any of his men wanted to be with local girls, they must first conduct a proper marriage ceremony.

George and Sâkis Tiigang were wed in an official Haida ceremony sometime in 1856, during which it is said they each wore a single white glove and linked hands to symbolize their union. Although mixed-race marriages were frowned upon in polite society, he brought her to Boston later that year for a Christian ceremony in the home of a local businessman. He built a house in Bellingham for his bride and, on December 31, 1857, she gave him a son, whom they named James "Jimmie" Tilton Pickett, after a good friend of George's. It was a difficult

JIMMIE PICKETT

George's first son, Jimmie, was a shy child with a talent for art. According to his guardian, Mrs. Collins, he used to make his own art materials from chunks of charcoal and the juice of berries. At the age of nineteen, he went to the Union Academy in Olympia, Washington, where he achieved high grades; but art was always his favorite subject, and he spent his spare time drawing landscapes and seascapes, people, and animals. He was given a job as artist for a local paper and had a painting of Bellingham Bay exhibited in a local gallery. However, he always yearned to become part of his father's family in Virginia, and waited in vain for the summons to travel east. He hated being mixed-race and didn't want to have children because "These crosses don't belong." He died of tuberculosis and typhoid at the age of thirty-two, with his father's cavalry sabre by his side.

ABOVE *Jimmie Pickett at the age of eighteen.*

delivery, though, and despite the attention of George's personal physician, Sâkis Tiigang never recovered. She died while her son was still a young baby.

George was distraught. He adored his Haida wife and couldn't believe he had lost a second wife to childbirth. For the next three years he devoted himself to looking after little Jimmie, only leaving him with his Native American grandmother if he had to travel on army duty. George loved the Washington countryside and seemed set to stay there had not the Civil War intervened.

When his home state of Virginia seceded from the Union, George had an impossible choice to make. He was an officer in the United States Army, and vehemently opposed to slavery, but his primary loyalties lay with Virginia. However, if he went to fight for the Confederate Army, who would look after his son? After much agonizing, in June 1861 he resigned from the U.S. Army and signed up for the Confederates. He asked a local couple, Catherine and William Collins, to bring up young Jimmie, promising to send financial support and gifts. He left three-year-old Jimmie a trunk containing the two white gloves his parents had worn at their wedding ceremony, along with a Bible bearing the inscription, "May the memory of your mother always remain dear. Your father, George E. Pickett."

Jimmie never saw him again.

The way to a man's heart

George was put in command of a brigade called the Gamecocks, in the Army of Northern Virginia. According to Sallie Corbell, his first letter to her was written in September 1861, and already the two sounded intimate: "How happy a certain captain . . . would be to look into your beautiful, soul-speaking eyes and hear your wonderfully musical voice," he wrote.

Sallie was the eldest of nine children and had grown up on a plantation in Suffolk, Virginia, where her parents were slave owners. She was a pupil at the Lynchburg Female Seminary, and a proper Southern lady, when her romance with George Pickett began (or was rekindled, depending on which version you believe) after he was stationed near Richmond. Over the next two years, he wrote to her regularly, and she visited him at his encampments. When she was in the neighborhood, he would slip off every evening to see her, much to the disapproval of his fellow officers.

"What a change love does make! How tender all things become to a heart touched by love."

Unlike most other officers, George seems to have written to Sallie in some detail about troop movements and battles fought, leading historians to question whether the letters were revised with hindsight by Sallie herself as part of her effort to rehabilitate her "Soldier." All the same, during those difficult war years it's clear that she was the bright spot in his life: "What a change love does make! How tender all things become to a heart touched by love."

George suffered a shoulder injury at the Battle of Gaines's Mill in June 1862, and was deeply moved when Sallie brought flowers to his bedside, promising to return "before they had wilted." At first the injury was thought to be slight, but in fact it put him out of action for three months, and for some time afterwards his arm was so stiff and painful that he was unable to get it into the sleeve of his jacket.

By April 1863, when the Southern army was planning to march north to confront the enemy on their own soil, George begged Sallie to come to his camp and marry him ahead of the confrontation they both knew was looming. He yearned for

BELOW
Heroic but ultimately doomed to failure: Pickett's Charge at Gettysburg on July 3, 1863, was a bloodbath.

the comfort of knowing that "if I fall I shall fall as your husband." But she had been raised too strictly to contemplate being married "by the wayside in that desultory and unstudied fashion," and asked him to "wait until a more favorable time." Two months later, his division crossed the Potomac and marched into Pennsylvania, coming to a halt a few miles from Gettysburg and the battle that would haunt George for the rest of his life.

Pickett's Charge

Union general John Buford ordered his men to take up position along the ridges west of Gettysburg to face off the advancing Confederate Army while waiting for reinforcements. On July 1, 1863, Confederate general Robert E. Lee attacked, but after two days of heavy fighting had been unable to force the Northern troops to retreat. George Pickett's division arrived at the end of the second day, and, at a strategy meeting that evening, Lee decided to launch a massive attack on the center of the Union line, which he believed had been weakened by the fighting. Three divisions, including Pickett's, were to lead the attack.

At 1 p.m. on July 3, Confederate cannons launched a great artillery barrage at the Union lines, unaware that the majority of their shells were missing their target and falling on the slopes

ABOVE
Confederate general Robert E. Lee: a Southern gentleman of the old school.

CIVIL WAR SONGS

George wrote to Sallie that as they marched through the town of Chambersburg, Pennsylvania, young ladies emerged from their houses and asked that the regimental bands play, so they struck up some old favorites such as "Home Sweet Home" and "Swanee." The ladies teased them for not playing "Dixie," which had become the Confederate anthem. Its lyrics tell of a freed slave yearning, rather implausibly, for the plantation on which he grew up, with "Dixie" being another name for the South. Other songs popular with the Confederates included "Stonewall Jackson's Way" and "Southern Soldier Boy." Both sides sang wistful songs, such as "When This Cruel War is Over" and "When Johnny Comes Marching Home." Survivors of Pickett's Charge at Gettysburg relate that bands stationed in the trees were playing martial songs as the troops set off into the field, and when the stragglers returned, the band struck up the hymn, "Nearer, My God, to Thee."

RIGHT
"One of the best tunes I ever heard," said Lincoln of "Dixie."

behind. At 3 p.m. the order was given for 13,000 Confederate soldiers to charge across open ground towards the center of the Union lines. Pickett shouted, "Up, men, and to your posts. Don't forget you are from old Virginia," and a line of men over a mile long stepped out with Confederate flags waving.

When they were about a third of the way across the open ground, Union artillerymen opened fire and mowed them down in their hundreds. It was a bloodbath. About 200 members of Pickett's division managed to reach Union lines and engaged in hand-to-hand fighting but they had no support from behind and were forced to retreat or surrender. Of Pickett's division of roughly 6,000 men, more than half were killed, wounded, or captured. Of his forty officers, twelve were killed, nine wounded, and five captured.

George Pickett himself survived and was later criticized for having led his men from well behind the front line, but at the time Lee took the blame, saying, "All this has been my fault." He asked Pickett to rally his division, to which George replied bitterly, "General Lee, I have no division."

The death toll at Gettysburg was unprecedented and shocked both sides, with around 23,000 Union casualties and a further 28,000 on the Confederate side. The Confederate march north was halted and General Lee would never again have the strength to go on the offensive.

George Pickett was personally devastated. He wrote to Sallie that were it not for her, "he would rather, a million times rather, be back there with his dead, to sleep for all time in an unknown grave." In an attempt to lift his spirits, Sallie crossed enemy lines and came to Petersburg to marry him in St Paul's Episcopal Church on September 15, from where they went on to Richmond for a brief honeymoon in the home of his sister.

Sallie then accompanied George back to his new post in Petersburg, claiming she wanted to check his "bad habits," such as drinking and swearing. She spent her time visiting hospitals with other officers' wives, and in July 1864 gave birth to George's son, George Junior.

A broken man

No one at the time condemned Pickett for his actions at Gettysburg, but when his men lost the crucial Battle of Five Forks on April 1, 1865, while he was having dinner two miles away, he was roundly criticized. The consensus was that while George was an excellent brigade commander, he was not up to managing a division. Some accounts say that he was relieved of his division command in the first week of April, but it seems he led his remaining troops at Appomattox Court House on April 9, the final battle of the war, and was with Robert E. Lee when the Confederate general surrendered.

ABOVE
George and Sallie on their wedding day. Even before their marriage he slipped away from camp to visit her most nights, according to his fellow officers.

BELOW
Confederate soldiers captured at Five Forks on April 1, 1865, while their commander was out at dinner.

NATIVE AMERICANS
IN THE CIVIL WAR

When war was declared, the area known as Indian Territory (modern-day Oklahoma), was inhabited by Native American tribes driven west by white settlers. Both sides in the war tried to attract them as volunteers, and the Confederates won the support of the Choctaw, Creek, Seminole, Catawba, and some Cherokee, with their promise of land treaties and the creation of a "Bureau for Indian Affairs." Other tribes, such as the Delaware, backed the Unionists, often acting as scouts for them, or joining "colored regiments" in which they were treated the same way as African-American soldiers. Union general James G. Blunt was responsible for bringing much of Indian Territory under Union control during the war. He raised the 1st Kansas Colored Infantry, the first multiracial unit to fight in the Civil War, and said of them, "Their coolness and bravery I have never seen surpassed."

Under the terms of the surrender, Pickett was paroled but not pardoned, and was briefly investigated for war crimes concerning an incident in 1864 in which 22 Union prisoners were executed in North Carolina, though charges were not pressed. He and Sallie fled to Montreal, Canada, where they lived for the best part of a year and had another son, David Corbell. In 1866, they returned to Virginia to try and earn a living, and George finally found work as an agent for Washington Life Insurance. He continued to send money for the upkeep of Jimmie, his son in Washington, but never attempted to see him even when he was in the area. By then, all his

loyalty lay with his new white family. A year before his death, in 1874, he was pardoned by the U.S. Congress for his role in the Civil War. In the same year, his youngest son, David, died of measles.

After the death of her "Soldier," Sallie was left short of money, before reinventing herself as a writer and speaker, particularly on the subject of the Civil War and what she saw as her husband's heroic role in it. She toured America, captivating audiences with her stories: "Enthusiasm over Mrs. Pickett's lecture on Gettysburg surpasses anything ever known here," wrote one Bostonian in 1910, and observed that it was the first time his fellow citizens had stood up when the band played "Dixie."

"*Enthusiasm over Mrs Pickett's lecture on Gettysburg surpasses anything ever known here.*"

But Sallie's version of George Pickett's life rewrote history in many respects, one of which was in removing any mention of his second wife, Sâkis Tiigang. She refused to accept that George had been married to a Haida woman, and claimed that Jimmie had merely been a gift from a local chief her husband had befriended. She wrote to Jimmie several times over the years, and when her husband died she sent him his cavalry sabre, but she wouldn't let him inherit the house his father had built in Bellingham until Jimmie threatened legal action.

Sallie was deeply depressed when her first son, George Jr., died of yellow fever in 1911, aged forty-seven, but she continued writing and touring right up until her own death in 1931, telling new generations her own stories of the old South, the Civil War, and the husband who to her was the hero of it all.

ABOVE
Mrs. George E. Pickett in 1887: author, public speaker, and eulogizer of her late husband.

OPPOSITE
Native Americans wounded during the Wilderness Campaign of May 1864.

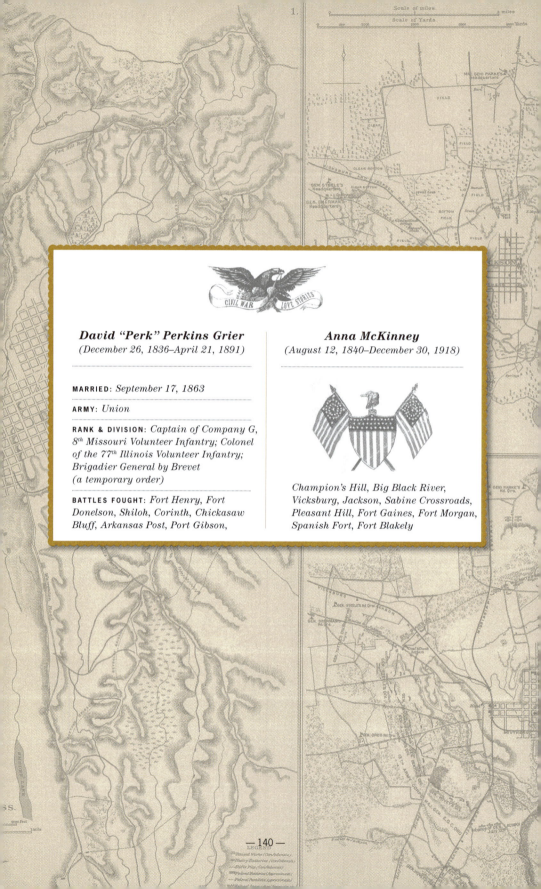

David "Perk" Perkins Grier
(December 26, 1836–April 21, 1891)

Anna McKinney
(August 12, 1840–December 30, 1918)

MARRIED: *September 17, 1863*

ARMY: *Union*

RANK & DIVISION: *Captain of Company G, 8th Missouri Volunteer Infantry; Colonel of the 77th Illinois Volunteer Infantry; Brigadier General by Brevet (a temporary order)*

BATTLES FOUGHT: *Fort Henry, Fort Donelson, Shiloh, Corinth, Chickasaw Bluff, Arkansas Post, Port Gibson,*

Champion's Hill, Big Black River, Vicksburg, Jackson, Sabine Crossroads, Pleasant Hill, Fort Gaines, Fort Morgan, Spanish Fort, Fort Blakely

Perk & Anna Grier

David P. Grier 1863

No 10

Franklin La. Nov 5th 1863
Thursday Night

My Very Dear Wife   To night it rains
very hard and I am shut up in
my Tent with nothing for company but
a perfect swarm of Musquetos and
a very severe spell of the Blues or
Homesickness.   I have been all evening
lying on my Cot thinking of Home and
of you and wishing I were this ought
with you. I tried to think what you
might be doing this evening but of course
I imagined a great many things you
might be at. but could not tell certain
by whether any of them were correct.
I finally concluded that I must do
something to shake of the feeling of lone=
liness that was creeping over me and

Perk and Anna had their fair share of jealousy, squabbles, and misunderstandings during the four long years of his military service, but there was never any doubt about the depth of their feelings for each other, or about their desire to be together for the rest of their days.

David Perkins Grier, known to his friends as "Perk," grew up in Danville, Pennsylvania in a solid Scots Presbyterian family. In 1851, when he was fifteen, the Griers moved to Peoria, Illinois, where his father established a grain business. Perk became close friends with David McKinney, whose family had also moved west from Pennsylvania to Peoria, and thus made the acquaintance of David's younger sister Anna.

Perk was a strikingly handsome young man who had been involved in several romantic entanglements with female admirers before young Anna caught his eye. Even after he and Anna began courting in 1860 or early 1861, she was cautious on account of her suspicions about other women in his life. He had been linked with a girl called Rose Stettinius, to whom he wrote and apologized, explaining that he hadn't meant to mislead her in any way. Despite this, Anna was concerned that Perk might still have feelings for Rose. Perk reassured Anna, "You know that I think the World and all of you and if you were lost to me I would not care for living." He was a romantic soul who wasn't afraid to express his feelings, and when he found out that Anna had "carried on a flirtation" with a man named Rob Strong, Perk wrote that he "felt real jealous of him."

Back in 1856, Perk had joined the National Blues, a militia company in Peoria, and straight after hostilities began in 1861, he tried to enlist, only to be turned away, as they had already reached their quota of recruits in Illinois. He then applied to Missouri, and was taken on as a captain in Company G of the 8th Missouri Volunteer Infantry. In early 1862 he was sent to one of the most volatile areas of fighting, along the Mississippi, and engaged in battle after bloody battle. It was only his correspondence with Anna that lifted his spirits. Every week he wrote professing his feelings, and most days he took out her picture for "a long good look." She was the bright spot in a war that quickly came to seem "disgusting."

OPPOSITE
Less than two months after their wedding, Perk was pining for his beloved Anna and poured out his feelings on paper, saying that he was "lying on my Cot thinking of Home and of you and wishing I were this night with you."

Calmness in battle

Perk saw his first battle on February 6, 1862, at Fort Henry, Tennessee, closely followed by another at Fort Donelson, from February 11 to 16. A man never really knows how he will cope until he has been in battle, but Perk wrote that "when the Bullets were flying the fastest, of one thing I am certain I did not feel the least fear." He had a strong feeling he was not going to be killed, although he saw many fall in battle around him. Still, at one point he felt moved to write to Anna that, "If it is my fate to be Killed in any of these actions my last thoughts shall be of you, and the last word spoken shall be your name."

By the end of March, the hardships of wartime and the stress of battle had taken their toll, and Perk tried to resign, but his resignation was rejected by his commander. He'd been ill with suspected typhoid, and still felt weak when he had to fight at the Battle of Shiloh in April, a fierce conflict in which there was heavy fighting for ten long hours, and the field, "six miles long + four broad," was "perfectly covered with dead and wounded." Both sides were shocked by the carnage, with Union casualties of 13,047 killed, wounded, or captured, and Confederate casualties of 10,725. Although there would be other battles with more severe death tolls, this was the first in which the soldiers fell in their thousands; for the participants it must have been horrifying.

Rather than sympathizing, Anna wrote a cold, distant letter to Perk in early May, pointing out to him that he couldn't expect gushing professions of love from her when they were not officially

> " *When the Bullets were flying the fastest, of one thing I am certain I did not feel the least fear.* "

BACKGROUND
The Battle of Fort Donelson, February 13–16, 1862: after it was lost, the Confederates could no longer defend Nashville.

ABOVE
*The Battle of Shiloh,
April 6–7, 1862:
it was won by the
Union's General Ulysses
S. Grant, but at great
cost in human lives.*

engaged. "You are the queerest girl," Perk wrote back, before assuring her that, should he live, he intended to marry her as soon as possible. "I now consider myself as fast bound as if I were married," he wrote. However, it seems that she may not have felt the same commitment, because she began to mention a "young gentleman" whom she had met during a trip to visit family in Shippensburg, Pennsylvania. Was she trying to make Perk jealous? "Do tell me all about it," he wrote back, "for my curiosity is very highly excited."

In July, he heard that Anna had visited the town of Elmwood, Illinois, and was concerned that his past romances in the area would reach Anna's ears and arouse her suspicions once more.

RUNAWAY SLAVES

From the early months of the war, Union commanders had to decide what to do with the large number of runaway slaves who approached them seeking safety. Until Lincoln's Emancipation Proclamation of January 1863, the law stated that they should be returned to their owners, but in practice Union officers made their own decisions about what to do with this "contraband of war." Some returned the slaves while others allowed them stay in special "contraband camps," where they did manual work for the army—digging trenches, doing laundry, or cooking for the troops—in return for minimal wages plus board and lodgings for them and their families. Missionaries who visited the camps were outraged by the conditions, but the sad fact was that for many African-Americans from the South they represented a good step up from slavery. By the end of the war there were more than one hundred contraband camps following the Union Army.

There was a "gay widow" with whom he confessed he used to pass the time, and another young lady, Miss Simpson, "whom reports used to say I was going to marry." Given Perk's womanizing past, is it any wonder that Anna found it hard to trust him and was often reserved with her own feelings?

At last, in a letter he received on July 10, she wrote that she loved him with all her heart. Of course, he was delighted, promising he would never trifle with her. She insisted that he burned all her letters (probably because she didn't want them to fall into enemy hands should he be killed or injured), and he agreed, saying it didn't matter because they were "indelibly impressed on my mind + heart."

A significant promotion

By the summer of 1862, the flush of patriotism with which Perk had signed up had "very nearly disappeared," and he was irked to find himself ineligible for promotion in the 8th Missouri because he was not from the regiment's home state. In August 1862 his father wrote to Abraham Lincoln requesting help in getting Perk transferred, and it seems from the tone that the two were acquainted: "I have been and allways will be your Friend," the letter concludes. The string-pulling worked, and Perk was commissioned as colonel of the newly

formed 77th Illinois Volunteer
Infantry—a huge promotion for him.
Anna's brother, David, would serve
with him as quartermaster.

It was a position of great trust, but
before long Perk had problems. The
77th Illinois quickly become known
as the "Abolition Regiment" because
of the anti-slavery views of its leaders.
This made them a target for runaway
slaves, many of whom sought refuge
with the 77th while they were in
Kentucky. Perk was strongly in favor
of abolition and refused to return
slaves to their owners, even though
Union general Andrew Jackson Smith
threatened him with arrest and court

"I always was too fast of speculating . . . and you know the Saying is such men never will get rich;"

martial. Perk stuck to his course, which he believed to be in line
with government rules, and the general later apologized. Needless
to say, Perk was in favor of Lincoln's Emancipation Proclamation,
and converted Anna to his views on the ills of slavery—though he
didn't succeed with her mother, who thought he was just wrong.

By December 1862, Perk and Anna were wearing each other's
rings, and he suggested their getting married so that she would be
able to visit him in camp. He warned her that he might never be
wealthy, saying, "I always was too fast of speculating . . . and you
know the Saying is such men never will get rich;" but still she
wanted to be his wife. On the 13th of the month he wrote to Anna's
parents to ask their permission, then had a long, anxious wait until
her father's reply came on February 3, 1863. Mr. McKinney agreed
to the wedding, but not while Perk remained in the army, which,
he said, was an "unsettling and itinerating position," because they
were frequently on the move and facing danger.

ABOVE
*There seem to have
been many women who
would have happily
accepted Perk's hand in
marriage, but he set his
sights on Anna and did
not give up until he had
won her.*

OPPOSITE
*A group of
"contrabands" near
Yorktown, Virginia:
free but still not equal.*

Perk then received a very depressing letter from his own
mother, who had spoken to Anna's mother and formed the
impression that she didn't think Perk a good enough match
for her daughter. Anna had had offers from three men wealthier
than him, his mother wrote, besides which he might come home
from the war "a cripple." He wrote to Anna yet again outlining
his financial position and saying he "never would come of the
field a cripple, it must be either sound + whole, or a corpse."

It took several letters and many more conversations to resolve
the impasse, but by April the McKinneys had changed their
position and the wedding was approved for later that year. Anna
and Perk then had a long negotiation about the wedding date,
which had to be arranged to coincide with a time when he could
get furlough. The engagement period was difficult for them both,
not least because they barely saw each other, and Anna worried
he would find her changed when they met again.

At last they became man and wife on September 17, 1863,
in what was acclaimed as "the most colorful and romantic event
of the nineteenth century in Peoria." They traveled east on their
honeymoon, staying for a while in New York before Perk had
to return to duty in mid-October. As they parted, she handed
him a note telling him how deeply she loved him, but both felt
miserable at the enforced separation. "I never in my life felt so
much like deserting," he wrote to her. "I am ready and willing
to give up everything to be with you."

Fighting in the Deep South

Throughout 1863 and most of 1864, Perk was engaged in battle
after battle. A false report was printed in the Peoria newspapers
on January 30, 1863 that he had been wounded at Vicksburg, and
he hastened to reassure Anna that this was not the case, though
he told her that he "came pretty near it at Arkansas Post." In May,
he was part of the army enforcing the siege of Vicksburg, then in
July he fought at the Battle of Jackson, Mississippi.

Perk had requested of his superiors that, once he and Anna
were wed, he should be posted to a town where his wife could
join him; in being sent to New Orleans in October 1863, his wish
was granted. The city had been captured by Union forces in 1862,
and Perk's regiment were to be responsible for its defence as
Confederate forces moved in from the west. Anna was able to join

OPPOSITE
*During the summer
of 1862, General
Grant's troops were
tasked with building
a canal to redirect
the Mississippi, so
ships could bypass
Vicksburg. However,
the city fell before it
could be completed.*

him there for prolonged periods throughout the remainder of the war, staying over during the winter of 1864–65. It would not have been a particularly pleasant time for her, as the towns-people were hostile towards their occupiers, and sometimes her husband was away for weeks on end, but when together they were at last able to live as a married couple.

The 77th Illinois were involved in the Red River Campaign of March to May 1864, under the command of Lieutenant Colonel Webb. The regiment suffered terrible losses, particularly in the Battle of Sabine Crossing, when 176 men were killed, wounded, or captured, leaving only 126 soldiers fit for active duty. During the Battle of Fort Morgan in August 1864, Perk was given command of the Union army, and in March 1865 he was temporarily promoted to brigadier general when he joined the army of Union general Canby for the march up to and capture of Mobile, Alabama. He was still fighting in the Battle of Fort Blakely on April 9, 1865, six hours after

THE SIEGE OF VICKSBURG

From May 22 through to July 4, 1863, Perk's regiment was part of the army laying siege to the town of Vicksburg. Citizens hid in dugouts excavated in the hillsides to avoid the Union bombardment, and as food became scarce they resorted to eating the meat of mules and even rats. They held out through June, hoping that a Confederate regiment would come to relieve them, but were forced to surrender when it became apparent that they wouldn't be rescued. Perk walked into the city on the day of the surrender and wrote to Anna that "scarcely a house had escaped having a shell put through them," and when he visited the caves dug in the hillsides, he found them full of women and children. Around 29,000 Confederates were captured, but Union general Grant was forced to set them free on parole because he couldn't manage the logistics of getting them all to distant Union prisons.

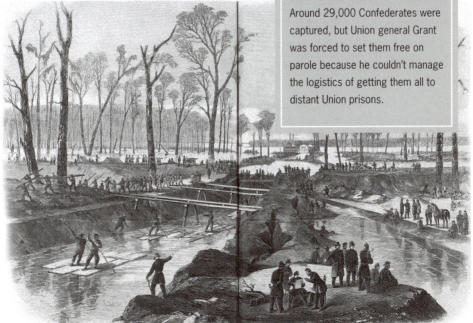

NEW ORLEANS

New Orleans was an early target for Union strategists because of its position at the mouth of the Mississippi and the fact that, with 168,675 inhabitants, it was the largest city in the Confederacy. After the naval forts surrounding it were captured, General Benjamin Butler's troops were able to march in on May 1, 1862. His rule over the occupied townspeople was deeply unpopular, though. According to his orders, anyone who called out in support of Confederate generals was sentenced to three months' hard labour; any woman who insulted Union troops was "treated as a woman of the town" (in other words, a prostitute); newspapers and religious sermons were censored; and a man named William Mumford was hanged for tearing down a Union flag. Butler, known to local residents as "the Beast," was reassigned in December, and by the time Perk reached the city in October 1863, relations were much improved though still tense.

ABOVE
Explosions lit the sky like fireworks when New Orleans was taken by night.

"*My heart is irrecoverably lost and it is yours, for ever*"

Robert E. Lee had surrendered, as Confederate troops continued to fire at them. In fact, Perk wasn't finally discharged and allowed to travel home until July. No one had fought a longer or harder war than him, yet he escaped without so much as a scratch.

Speculating in grain

Perk and Anna set up home in Peoria and wasted no time in starting a family, with the first of their seven children born in 1866. Perk established a grain business with his brother Robert, and together they were responsible for building the first grain elevator in Peoria. In 1879 they moved to St. Louis, where the two brothers attempted to corner the market in grain; but, as he had warned Anna before they married, Perk was prone to speculation, and his business collapsed, taking with it the family fortune. He tried to recover his losses, starting two further companies, but was never able to reestablish the standard of living he wished for Anna and his children.

Following Perk's death in 1891, after a year-long illness, Anna remained in St. Louis for a further twenty-five years, and she must often have enjoyed rereading the beautiful wartime letters she'd received from her dashing husband: "My heart is irrecoverably lost and it is yours, for ever," he had written, telling her that when they were together he would feel "perfectly contented Knowing that I have just the best young Lady in the land."

Perk's obituary in the local Peoria press: he had survived more battles than most and become a local hero. "I was Not Born to be Shot," he once wrote to Anna.

weeks ago ... at h ... ing health sufficiently to b ... bed. At the time of his death ... Grier was surrounded by his family, consisting of a wife, five sons and two daughters.

At the outbreak of the war General David P. Grier was engaged in business at Elmwood, Ill. As soon as he heard of the fall of Fort Sumter he expressed his determination to enter the service. He at once began recruiting a company, and the ranks were soon full, when he was elected Captain. He tendered the services of himself and the company to Governor Yates of Illinois, but as the State quota was already full his services were not accepted. He then took his company to St. Louis, where they were mustered into the service in June, 1861, as Co. G, Eighth, Missouri Volunteer Infantry. As Captain of that company he was actively engaged for several months, participating in the battles of Fort Henry, Fort Donelson, Shiloh, and the siege and capture of Corinth, Miss., besides many skirmishes of minor importance.

On the 25th of August, 1862, Captain Grier was ordered to report to Springfield, Ill., for orders. On arriving there he was commissioned by Governor Yates as Colonel of the Seventy-seventh Illinois Volunteer Infantry, September 2, and was mustered in on the 12th of the same month. He was in command of his regiment continuously from that time until the surrender of Vicksburg, July 4, 1863. During the seige of Jackson, Miss., and until the return to Vicksburg he was in command of the brigade to which the Seventy-seventh belonged. At Franklin and New Iberia, La., November, 1863, he commanded the Second Brigade, Fourth Division, Thirteenth Army Corps. In August, 1864, he was placed in command of all the land forces on Dauphine Island, Alabama, under orders of Major-General Granger, who commanded the expedition. After the capture of Fort Gaines all the troops on the island, excepting the Seventy-seventh and one other regiment, crossed over to the peninsula and laid siege to Fort Morgan. Colonel Grier was ordered over with them and retained command of the land forces until the surrender of Fort Morgan. On March 26, 1865, Colonel Grier was commissioned Brevet Brigadier-General, a promotion well earned by four years of faithful service; and too long withheld. When General Canby organized the expedition against Mobile in the spring of 1865, General Grier was assigned to duty on his brevet rank and ordered to command the First Brigade during the entire campaign against Mobile, and the assaults upon Spanish Fort and Blakely, and also after the capture of Mobile on the march up the Tombigbee River. On the return from that march he was assigned to the command of the Third Division, Thirteenth Army Corps, and remained in command of that division until he and his regiment were mustered out, July 10, 1865.

The remains will be interred at Peoria, Ill., and will leave St. Louis for their last resting place at 7:45 o'clock this evening, accompanied by delegations from Ransom Post of the Grand Army, the Loyal Legion and from the Merchants' Exchange. The deceased was about 53 years of age. He was a son of John Grier of Peoria, Ill., who is over 83 years of age, and who is still vigorous.

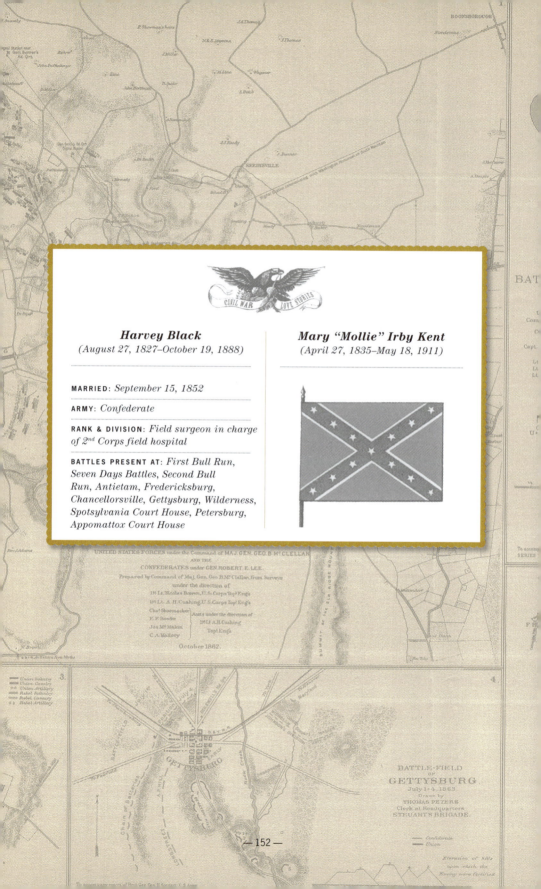

Harvey Black
(August 27, 1827–October 19, 1888)

Mary "Mollie" Irby Kent
(April 27, 1835–May 18, 1911)

MARRIED: *September 15, 1852*

ARMY: *Confederate*

RANK & DIVISION: *Field surgeon in charge of 2ⁿᵈ Corps field hospital*

BATTLES PRESENT AT: *First Bull Run, Seven Days Battles, Second Bull Run, Antietam, Fredericksburg, Chancellorsville, Gettysburg, Wilderness, Spotsylvania Court House, Petersburg, Appomattox Court House*

Harvey & Mollie Black

Harvey Black saw the worst of the war's carnage up close, yet most of his letters to his wife Mollie are chatty and optimistic. He knew she was suffering from depression, and perhaps that's why he was careful to keep from her the awful realities of life on the front line.

By all accounts, Harvey Black was a quiet, thoughtful man, not given to huge outpourings of emotion, but one Sunday evening, November 1, 1863, when he had already been away from home for two and a half years, he wrote a sublime love letter to his wife, in which, writing in the third person, he relives their early courtship. He described meeting her in 1844 in a village in Western Virginia, when he was seventeen years old and she just eight. Despite the age difference, he says he was "favorably impressed" by her "fair face and gentle manners." Three or four years passed before he met her again and realized that the pretty little girl was blossoming into a beautiful woman, while the gap in their ages was becoming less significant.

After studying medicine at the University of Virginia, in 1849 he traveled out West looking for a place to set up home, even buying some property in Wisconsin. But he didn't find a town to suit him and that, plus memories of Mollie, induced him to return. Back in

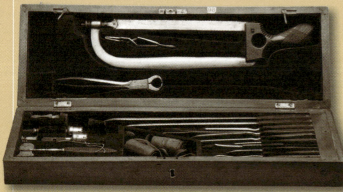

ABOVE
A surgeon's operating case: The large oval tool at the top is a bone saw, and beneath that is a type of grip used for extracting bullets.

Virginia, he began to seek out her company, and, as he described in his letter to her in November 1863, "I would pass an hour or two in the enjoyment of her company with great pleasure to myself." Meanwhile, he managed to set up a medical practice in Blacksburg and strove to make himself "a fair reputation." At last, after much coyness, Mollie accepted his proposal of marriage and, writing many years later from the front, he remarked, "the years increase the affection & esteem we have for each other."

In Mollie's reply she teased him, saying that if he thought her so fair of face why did he not carry her likeness around with him? He told her it was too precious to risk being damaged. They may have been married eleven years and had four children by that point, but it seems the romance was still very much alive.

> *"I would pass an hour or two in the enjoyment of her company with great pleasure to myself."*

Relatives in the North

The town of Blacksburg, Virginia, had been founded in 1798 by Harvey Black's grandfather and great uncle, and he had plenty of kinsfolk in the area, but in 1854 his parents, brothers, and sister moved to Wisconsin, where they set up home in the property Harvey had bought there. Mollie's mother originally came from Blacksburg, but her father was born in Connecticut and her relatives were split between Illinois, Wisconsin, and Missouri. This geographical spread meant that when the Civil War began in April 1861, Harvey and Mollie both had close relatives in the North—and some, including her younger brother Lewis, volunteered to fight for the Unionist cause.

BELOW
The University of Virginia, where Harvey Black studied medicine, in 1845.

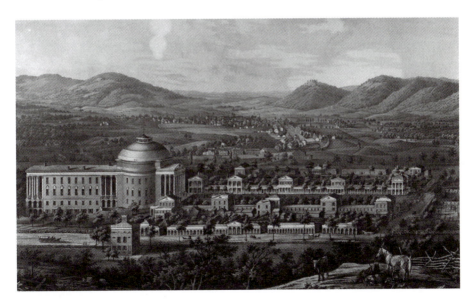

RIGHT
Surgeons of the 3ʳᵈ corps outside a hospital tent. Field stations were set up between half a mile and a mile behind the front line.

It must have been hard for them when they heard this news, as both were patriotic Southerners convinced of the righteousness of Secession. Harvey was pleased that none of his own brothers signed up, but wrote to Mollie about Lewis, "His active temperament together with the fact that his uncle (no doubt conscientiously) has aided to impress his mind with the wrongfulness of slavery has made him feel free to enlist." At the time, Harvey and Mollie kept one slave, a girl called Adeline, who at least seems to have been well-treated. Certainly, when she was ill, Harvey suggested his wife took her to the local doctor to get a prescription—something many slave owners would not have done. Their Northern relatives had hardened their views against slavery, though, and Harvey and Mollie decided not to have any contact with them for the duration of the war. But whenever Harvey visited hospitals with wounded Yankee prisoners, he kept an eye out for his brother-in-law.

Harvey enlisted as regimental surgeon with the Fourth Virginia Infantry, which saw action at the Battle of Bull Run, the first battle of the war, and he was thrown in at the deep end, dealing with the horrific casualties of that encounter. He became assistant surgeon to Dr. Hunter McGuire, the medical director of the Army of Northern Virginia, and himself had an assistant called John Samuel Apperson, whom he helped to train. Together the three of them would deal with casualties from some of the bloodiest battles of the war as they followed Stonewall Jackson's brigade and then the army of Robert E. Lee. Harvey performed hundreds of amputations during the course of the war and assisted Dr. McGuire when Jackson's arm was amputated.

A family man

When he went to war, Harvey's oldest child, Kentie, was eight and his youngest, Charly, was two; by the time he came back the children were aged between twelve and six. He often wrote about them in his letters to Mollie, saying, "I feel mighty proud of them . . . I don't think I would be half so good a soldier if I did not have so many little fellows to fight for." But being at war meant he missed out on many milestones: in one letter he expressed sorrow at the fact that he had not yet heard little Charly talk.

Mollie stayed in Blacksburg where she home-schooled her children. During the month of April 1864, three years after the war began, eleven-year-old Kentie went to visit his father at a camp in Orange County, Virginia, and Harvey wrote back very impressed by his son's education: "He reads better than expected," he said, and "I can already see the benefit derived in the lessons he has taken in mental arithmetic." In some ways he was a protective father, letting Kentie share his narrow army cot at night rather than making him sleep in a bed of his own, but he didn't conceal from his son the brutality of war, on one occasion letting him watch the execution of a deserter. Perhaps he thought it was his duty to educate the boy in the realities of the world while his mother concentrated on academic subjects. At any rate, father and son appear to have become close during the trip.

Back in Blacksburg, Mollie struggled to get meat, coffee, and shoes for her children. She had money, because her husband regularly

RAMPANT INFLATION

After Unionist ships blockaded Southern ports in the summer of 1861 and the Confederates were no longer able to export cotton, the entire economy was forced to change overnight. More grain was planted, but the army got priority when food was distributed, and it soon began to run short on the home front. The Confederate government adopted a policy of printing money, but this led to spiralling inflation. They then issued Confederate bonds, promising that the government of the South would redeem them. But the measure only helped in the short term, and by the war's end bonds were useless. In 1863, wheat cost three times what it had at the start of the war, and butter and milk cost four times as much, while salt became unaffordable to all but the wealthiest. In April 1863, thousands of women rioted in Richmond over the lack of food. They looted stores and only went home when Jefferson Davis threatened that his militia would shoot them.

BELOW *In 1863, this 75-cent note would only buy half a pound of butter.*

BATTLEFIELD SURGERY

Every regiment had a surgeon and an assistant surgeon, armed with scalpels, saws, chisels, bone cutters, and all manner of gruesome devices. The powerful new breech-loading repeating rifles caused ragged, gaping wounds and the only treatment for severe injuries to arm or leg was amputation to prevent gangrene and septicemia. Ether or chloroform were administered to anesthetize the patient, but instruments were not disinfected—hands weren't even washed, because the importance of hygiene was not yet recognized—so secondary infections often set in. The success of an operation depended on several factors, but the speed at which the patient could be operated on was crucial. After some battles, men lay in agony on the field for days, and their chances of survival were severely decreased. Overall, one in four amputations resulted in the death of the patient.

sent cash, but it became increasingly difficult to procure many goods, as the Northern blockade took effect and prices became inflated. Her husband often wrote to her about friends and neighbors of theirs who had been wounded or killed, so towns-people would visit Mollie to hear the latest news. She enjoyed the company, but there were days when she saw no one apart from her children: "This has been a long, lonesome day to me. I have not even been to the front door," she wrote to Harvey in the depths of winter.

It's not clear when depression took hold of Mollie, but her husband referred to it in a letter of April 1862: "Don't get low spirited. There never was a war but this that ended at some time, and this will do so too." In November 1863, he wrote that he hoped she had got over her

> *"Last night we all slept in our clothes, expecting the Yankees in every moment."*

"attack of the Blues." But she had good reason to be depressed and anxious, as the list of acquaintances killed began to mount and rumors spread that the Union Army could be at the door any day. On December 18, 1863, she wrote, "Last night we all slept in our clothes, expecting the Yankees in every moment." It must have been terrifying for her. Bad news followed bad news for Southerners, as key towns fell to the North, and it became harder for her husband to reassure her that he regarded "ultimate success as sure."

Life as a field medic

Being in the medical team might have been safer than being an infantryman, but it wasn't an easy option. Mobile field hospitals were set up about half a mile to a mile behind the front, but medics often found themselves in the line of fire if troops retreated. When the wounded were brought off by stretcher bearers, they were first of all assessed at a field station, where emergency first aid could be administered, then transported in wagons back to the field hospital, which was situated in a suitable house, hotel, barn, warehouse, or local school. If patients needed longer-term care, they were transferred to a regular hospital in the area, or billeted in private homes (often the safer option, away from the risk of exposure to infectious diseases carried by other

OPPOSITE
Tending a wounded soldier in a field hospital: conditions were unsanitary and infection rates high.

— 159 —

patients). For both sides, a solid red flag marked the field station where ambulances and first aid were located, while a yellow flag with a dark green "H" on it marked field hospitals and general hospitals. Those who died in hospitals and prisons could expect a decent burial, but close to the front line the dead were simply wrapped in blankets and placed in hurriedly dug common graves.

Harvey was a doctor first and a Confederate second, as became clear after the Battle of Chancellorsville, from which he wrote to Mollie, "I was in several of the Hospitals where the wounded Yankees were and had about 28 under my care." If a man needed help he would give it, regardless of cause or color.

When Southern troops captured the town of Winchester in May 1862, they found dozens of wounded Unionist soldiers being treated in the Union Hotel hospital. According to J. Burd Peale, the Union surgeon in charge, Harvey Black came to see him and insisted he continue to care for the sick and wounded men. As the number of patients increased, Harvey let Peale have 64 Union prisoners of war to help him in his work. Then at the end of the month, Harvey and his boss, Hunter McGuire, signed a document giving the Union medics parole as prisoners of war. It was a humanitarian breakthrough, and the Union surgeons immediately pledged to use their influence to campaign for the release of Confederate surgeons being held in prisoner-of-war camps. The practice of treating medics as non-combatants was a major step forward, and has been hailed as a precursor of the modern International Committee of the Red Cross.

BELOW
Carrying wounded off the field at the Battle of Chancellorsville, May 1863.

OPPOSITE
A graveyard in Blacksburg, Virginia. On the tombstone of a local Civil War colonel, Charles B. Ronald, are the words "I have suffered."

THE BLOODIEST BATTLES OF THE WAR

BATTLE	CONFEDERATE CASUALTIES*	UNIONIST CASUALTIES*
Gettysburg	28,063	23,049
Chickamauga	18,454	16,170
Spotsylvania Court House	13,421	18,399
Chancellorsville	13,303	17,197
Wilderness	11,125	17,916
Antietam	13,724	12,410
Shiloh	10,725	13,047
Stone's River	10,266	13,249
Second Bull Run	8,350	13,830
Fort Donelson	15,067	2,331

* These figures include those killed, wounded, taken prisoner, and reported missing. Exact totals vary from source to source.

Despite his humanitarian work, Harvey was still determined that the Confederates should prevail, writing in 1862, "whip them we can, and whip them we will." But by 1863, particularly after Gettysburg, it must have been harder to maintain the optimistic tone. Instead of describing defeats in battle or the mounting numbers of casualties, he wrote to Mollie on subjects such as General Early's view that men should not get married during wartime, and that women should not visit army camps. The tone is remarkably light for a man who spent his waking hours sawing off limbs, his clothes spattered in blood, with the smell of rotting flesh in his nostrils while listening to the ear-splitting cries of men in mortal agony. Mentally, he must have been remarkably strong.

The end is near

BELOW
In April 1865, fleeing Confederate troops set fire to warehouses in Richmond, and the fire spread out of control, destroying large parts of the city.

Richmond, the Southern capital, was captured by Union troops on April 3, 1865, while Robert E. Lee's army retreated westward, pursued by the enemy. Mollie Black must have been petrified as town after town in Virginia was overrun by Unionists. Reports must have reached her of the trail of devastation being wrought by General Sherman's forces in Georgia, though in the end Blacksburg was not invaded.

Lee's army was finally trapped by Northern forces near the village of Appomattox Court House, and he had no choice but to surrender on April 9. Harvey Black was there at the time, and was one of the witnesses present on April 12, 1865,

"The joys of wedlock pass not away with the 'honeymoon', but daily give increasing and more refined happiness as time glides on."

when the aristocratic Robert E. Lee, in full dress uniform and carrying an antique silver sword, met Ulysses S. Grant, dressed in mud-spattered private's uniform, to agree terms. Harvey must have been heartened by their clemency, particularly the order that all combatants could go home without punishment, and the promise that 25,000 rations would be distributed to starving Confederate soldiers.

Harvey was extremely lucky to come out of the war unscathed, and Mollie must have been overjoyed when he made his way back to Blacksburg and walked in the front door of their home. It must have been difficult to adjust to civilian life after four years away, witnessing the most horrific suffering imaginable, but Harvey appears to have coped well, going back to work in his medical practice and rapidly becoming a pillar of the community. In 1872, he was appointed president of the Medical Society of Virginia, and the same year he helped to found the Virginia Agricultural and Mechanical College. Three years later, he was surprised when asked to become superintendent of the Eastern Lunatic Asylum in Williamsburg, having no formal training in psychology; nevertheless, he held the post for six years. He also sat as a Democrat in the Virginia House of Delegates and used his influence to have a new mental hospital built.

However, by 1887 he was suffering from the symptoms of prostate cancer. His old colleague Hunter McGuire operated twice, but he died in October 1888. Mollie survived him by twenty-three years, during which time she was present at the wedding of her only daughter Lizzie to Harvey's wartime colleague John Samuel Apperson. Perhaps she shared with the newlyweds some of the beautiful sentiments her husband had written to her about marriage in his frequent letters from the front, such as "The joys of wedlock pass not away with the 'honeymoon', but daily give increasing and more refined happiness as time glides on."

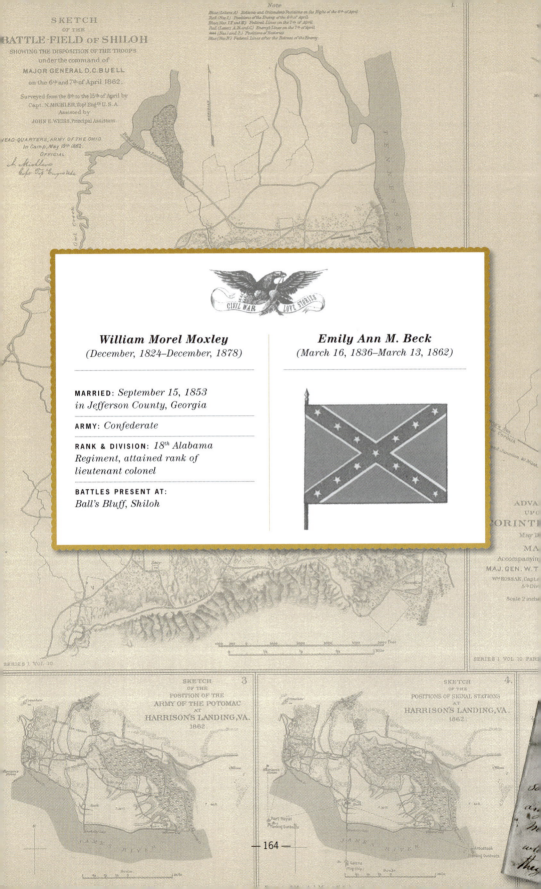

William Morel Moxley
(December, 1824–December, 1878)

Emily Ann M. Beck
(March 16, 1836–March 13, 1862)

MARRIED: *September 15, 1853 in Jefferson County, Georgia*

ARMY: *Confederate*

RANK & DIVISION: *18th Alabama Regiment, attained rank of lieutenant colonel*

BATTLES PRESENT AT: *Ball's Bluff, Shiloh*

William & Emily Moxley

W M Moxley   Bollock Ala Sept 8 1861

9 aclock ... Dear Husband it is now 8 ...

Page 1

Camp Johnson Sept 7

E. A. M. Moxley   My dear Wife it is a great blessing to those who have absent Relatives & friends to be in pos= =sefion of means of Communication by such a blesing we can communic[ate] all our thoughts & desires which is a great satisfaction to me nothing but your presence & to hear your talk but prefoable I Received a letter from you by mail this morning Sept 1st I was scarcly through reading of it before Mr Jones gave another backed by A. H. Justice to unmoder[ate] delight I found on opening of ... Emily but I ...

"The Democrat," a local paper in Huntsville, Alabama, urged its female readers not to write "gloomy letters" to their relatives in uniform, but Emily Moxley couldn't suppress the anxiety she felt on being left at home with five children to care for and another on the way.

William and Emily were a Southern farming couple who didn't own slaves, and there's little evidence in their letters of the patriotic support for the Confederate cause that marked the correspondence of some of their compatriots. They weren't particularly religious either, despite hailing from an area where there tended to be a church of one sort or another on virtually every street corner. Their prime concern was for each other and their immediate family, and all they wanted was for the conflict to end so they could be together once more.

William's parents were tenant farmers who moved around from place to place. It was while they were based in Georgia that he is likely to have met Emily Beck, whose parents owned a farm in Muscogee County. By then, William had bought his own small farm in Coffee County, Alabama. He described himself as a physician, although it's not clear whether he had any formal medical qualifications; he certainly didn't practice medicine at this time.

William was twelve years older than Emily and perhaps not the husband that her better-off family had in mind for their sixteen-year-old daughter. For some reason the couple weren't wed until September 1853, by which time they already had a son, George Edwin Moxley, who'd been born the previous December. It may be that Emily's parents tried to stop the marriage, and that it took the birth of a grandchild to persuade them to let it proceed.

Middle-class Southern women were used to being looked after by their menfolk, and weren't raised to know how to tend hogs, plough fields, or do the accounts. Emily's parents had four slaves who toiled on the land and in the family home, and she'd been brought up not expecting to lift a finger on her husband's farm; but she loved William and settled down enthusiastically to her role as wife and mother. She certainly had her work cut out: after George, first Mary J. Elizabeth (known as Betty) was born

OPPOSITE
The Halt (The Drink of Water) *by Thomas Nast, 1866. Nast worked as a battlefield artist and correspondent for* Harper's Weekly *during the war. This image shows a tired Union soldier begging for some water from a farmer's wife.*

in 1855, then Laura in 1856, Willie in 1858, and David in 1860, making Emily the mother of five children under the age of five when she was still only twenty-four years old—surely enough of a handful for anyone!

An unsafe pair of hands

On January 11, 1861, Alabama seceded from the Union and William Moxley decided that he must do his duty for his state, so he set about raising the Bullock Guards from the region of Coffee County where their farm was situated. His men elected him Captain on July 4 that year, and on the 25th of that month he received orders from General Lee to march with his company to Auburn, Alabama, where they would become part of the 18th Alabama Regiment.

He'd had six months to discuss with his wife how she would manage during his absence, and they decided that his brother Newton would supervise work on the farm, while William sent detailed instructions in his letters on everything from animal husbandry to childcare. Some Southern women went out to work or to farm the land themselves in their husbands' absence, but for Emily Moxley this wasn't an option, not only because of her middle-class background, but because by the time William left she was pregnant with their sixth child.

William's brother Newton had studied medicine in Florida and at the Reform Medical College in Macon, Georgia, and by the outbreak of war he was practicing as a doctor in New Providence, Alabama. It seems the last thing he wanted was to take responsibility for his older brother's farm, and soon Emily was complaining that he was withholding money William had sent for her, and that he was no help at all in getting some corn she was owed by a neighbor. On October 28 she wrote, "It looks like he is very tired of me and the children. A ready he is not willing to do anything for me and them."

As the months went by, Emily was forced to take some decisions about household management herself but she always anxiously relayed them to William: "I bought 4 meat hogs ... for 13 dollars, which I promised to pay as soon as possible. They will weigh 100 punds a piece." She was isolated, many miles

> *"I bought 4 meat hogs . . . for 13 dollars, which I promised to pay as soon as possible."*

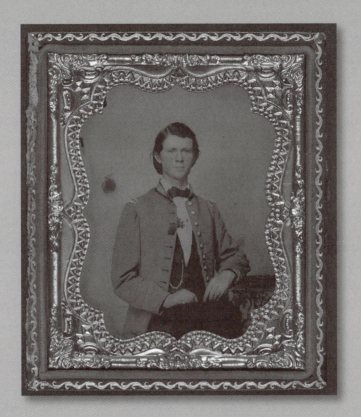

SOUTHERN VOLUNTEERS

At the outbreak of war, the South didn't have an army, but there were some state militias, and popular outrage against the North led thousands of idealistic young men to volunteer. At first they signed up for a year, but in December 1861 they were offered inducements to continue: 60 days of leave, a cash bonus, and the right to elect officers. It wasn't until April 1862 that compulsory military service was introduced for white men aged eighteen to thirty-five, and the following September this was extended to those up to forty-five. Controversially, planters with twenty or more slaves were exempt, and those wealthy men who didn't have twenty slaves could buy their way out of service by paying someone else to take their place. The going rate was $300, and it wasn't long before it became clear that if you valued your life, this would be money well-spent.

ABOVE
*Many were proud to wear the Confederate
frock coat and stand up for their ideals.*

RIGHT
*Others took advantage of any loophole to
buy their way out of war service.*

away from her husband and her birth family, without a male relative she could rely on, and having to do the best she could to feed her children.

All that kept her going were letters from her husband, which always contained lavish endearments. On September 1 he wrote, "I find nothing for my mind so salutary in effect as contemplating on the Object of my Effection. Dear Emily, I thought how often I have asked you to walk of an evening into the Guarden, but, Oh, when you think of those pleasant hours, or at least pleaseant to me, and you absent, it casts a shadow over evry thing else." She was equally affectionate in reply. On September 3 she wrote, "You told me to comb my hair ever time I thought of you. That is out of my power, for I would do nothing but comb it, for there is not one minute in the day but what I think of you."

BELOW
The task of collecting and burying the dead was usually given to those who weren't fit for battle.

"I find nothing for my mind so salutary in effect as contemplating on the Object of my Effection."

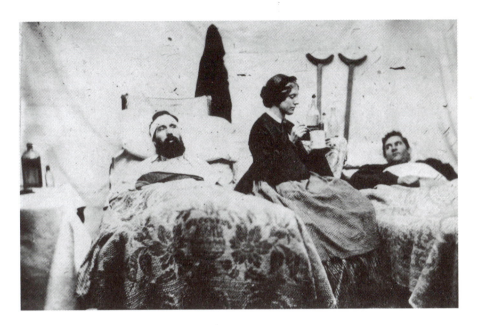

The 18th Alabama

William's regiment camped in Auburn for the summer of 1861
while undergoing basic training, where their greatest enemy
wasn't the Union Army but disease. Many of the men had come
from very small farming communities where they hadn't been
exposed to common diseases such as measles, mumps, smallpox, and scarlet fever, and thus they had no immunity from them.
On September 1, William reported that one man had died of measles,
and then there was a gap of several weeks in his letters. The lack
of news must have driven Emily wild with anxiety until, in mid-
October, she heard from a friend that William himself was sick.

Emily wrote several anguished letters during this period,
pouring out her fears. She was unable to sleep and, when she
did, she had nightmares about her husband's illness. It must have
been a huge relief when she received his letter of October 25
saying that he was improving slowly. It's obvious that he was
trying to calm her, but still he wrote of severe headaches and
extreme weakness. Once, on emerging from a delirious state,
he found that a purse containing all his money had been stolen,
and resolved that he would pursue the thief just as soon as he
was able. But, despite such presence of mind, it's not clear
whether he was strong enough to take part in the Battle of Ball's

ABOVE
*Thousands of women
in both the North and
South volunteered as
nurses to care for the
sick and wounded.*

DOCTORS' ORDERS

More than twice as many men died in the Civil War from disease as on the battlefield. The biggest killer was typhoid, spread by poor sanitation, with dysentery and malaria close behind. Opium, castor oil, and Epsom salts were used to treat diarrhea, as physicians believed in purging the system, but such drastic "cures" would likely have killed as many as they saved. Emily Moxley's brother Tom succumbed to typhoid and the doctor treated him with ten drops of turpentine every two hours, a herb called crawley root that induced sweating, a strong pepper poultice, some quinine, and Culver's root, a purging herb. After several weeks of this, Tom died in January 1862. During his last day of life the doctor gave him lobelia, which stimulates respiration but meant that he spent his final hours vomiting violently.

PILULÆ
QUINIÆ
SULPHATIS.
ch containing three grains o
Sulphes of quinia.
PREPARED AT THE
U. S. A.
MEDICAL PURVEYING DEPOT
ASTORIA, L. I.

LEFT
Quinine sulphate was effective against malaria but not without its side effects.

Bluff, in which his regiment fought on October 21, although he did write later, "We had a fight in Virginia which resulted in the defeat of the Yankees well."

It seems probable that William Moxley was suffering from malaria, because his illness recurred in November with three days of fever that left him weak and unsteady. The treatment recommended for malaria was quinine dissolved in a shot of whiskey, but as this was also prescribed for several other diseases including rheumatism, diarrhea, neuralgia, and syphilis, it may not have filled the patient with confidence of a good recovery. It also can't have helped Emily's state of mind when her brother wrote to her, "We have one of the sarriest [sorriest] Doctors for our batalion that you ever saw. He cant tell the chill and fever from the head ache."

It was December before William was well enough to move to his regiment's new camp at Mobile, Alabama, to settle in for the winter. There was a shortage of tents, but the men set about building cabins for winter quarters. While there, he managed to identify the soldier who had stolen his money as one Bill Kelly. All but 30 dollars of at least 120 had been spent—to put this in perspective, a soldier's pay was only 11 dollars a week. William arranged to have the remainder stopped from Bill Kelly's wages and the culprit was later court-martialed and drummed out of the army.

The Moxleys had financial troubles, as the men's wages were slow to be paid, and food and supplies were already starting to run scarce. A neighbor stole some of Emily's hogs, or so she suspected, and a near neighbor and close friend of hers died in childbirth. By the end of 1861, both she and her husband, though hundreds of miles apart, had sunk into a state of extreme despair and hopelessness. She wrote, "God grant

that we may live to meet in this life one time more."
He replied, bemoaning "this unholy war," which
was every day making widows and orphans and
"making the happiest homes desolate."

Childbirth in wartime

Emily begged William to come home for a
visit, but all leave was canceled as Ulysses
S. Grant's army marched into Tennessee in
February 1862. William and Emily discussed
whether she would be fit enough to come and
see him in camp, but decided it was unwise,
given the advanced state of her pregnancy.
After Grant took Forts Henry and Donelson
in February 1862, it was clear that Nashville
could no longer be defended, so Confederate
forces withdrew to concentrate their forces
at Corinth, Mississippi. The plan was to
launch a counter-offensive from there.

> " God grant that we may
> live to meet in this life
> one time more. "

Emily's baby was due in March, and she
knew she was unlikely to get much help in
childbirth as all medical personnel were at
the front lines of the war. It's no wonder she
was nervous. According to the 1850 census,
even with a doctor in attendance one in twenty-five white
women in the South died in childbirth—double the mortality
rate in the North. The fact that they tended to have larger families
was probably the main reason, with Southern wives having an
average of 5.5 live children each, though other factors against
them included the remoteness of some rural communities, which
made it difficult to get help.

Emily wrote often to her husband during these weeks, but
letters went astray and she appears to have heard little back from
him. The mule that delivered the mail in Coffee County had died,
railway bridges had been destroyed in battle, and really it was a
miracle that any letters got through at all. She received one on
February 24 that had been written on the 7th of that month, and
straightaway she sat down to reply. She wrote that she'd heard
a rumor that William had been put under guard in his camp for
some misdemeanor; it was completely untrue. In fact, he had been

promoted to second major the previous December and was obviously highly thought of in his regiment, which had now become part of the new Army of the Mississippi.

On March 10, Emily heard from her brother-in-law Newton that William had moved at short notice to Corinth. She replied, asking Newton to let her husband know that she and all the family were well, since it appeared her letters were not getting through. She felt very uneasy about her husband—presumably she knew the two armies were drawing close to each other near Corinth and that confrontation was imminent—but said she would try to write to him there.

And then, on March 13, Emily died while giving birth to her sixth child. The baby died too. There is no record of the exact cause of death but common causes included hemorrhaging, or sepsis caused by the use of unsterilized instruments and unwashed hands.

> "My dear Son, I write you a few lines to let you know you have a Father who loves you dearly."

Word was slow to reach William at his camp in Corinth, but on April 2 he wrote a heartbreaking letter to his eldest son George, who was nine years old: "My dear Son, I write you a few lines to let you know you have a Father who loves you dearly." He told him to be a good boy, to look after his little sisters and brothers, and to do as his grandparents asked him. "I do hope to see you before a great while," he finished. It must have been one of the most difficult letters any man could ever have to write.

Looking after the little ones

William Moxley was still with his regiment when they fought in the first day of the Battle of Shiloh at Pittsburgh Landing, but he doesn't appear to have gone out onto the field of battle. Perhaps his commander took pity on him, given his recent bereavement. Perhaps at the age of thirty-eight he was judged too old for the daring surprise attack on a Unionist camp that sparked the conflict. Those not considered battleworthy were often given the job of collecting the wounded from the field, which was only marginally less dangerous than fighting. At any rate, William was fortunate to escape Shiloh, the bloodiest battle of the war to date, with more than 23,000 men left dead, wounded or captured after two days of fighting on April 6 and 7. The 18th Alabama alone sent out 420 men, of whom 125 were either killed or wounded.

On April 21, 1862, William Moxley was allowed to resign from the army and came back to look after his five children. He put his farm up for sale and opened a shop selling groceries and general goods: everything from meat and molasses to kettles and shoes. Perhaps this was one way of helping to keep his children fed and clothed during the difficult remaining years of the war, but it may also have helped him to get an exemption when compulsory conscription was introduced in September that year.

In the late 1860s, he married Martha E. Justice, the widow of a friend, and by 1870 they were living in Texas with his and Emily's children and a new baby. All the evidence is that William was as caring a father as he had always been a husband to his beloved Emily.

BACKGROUND
The 18th Alabama was in the thick of the fighting on April 6, 1862, the first day of the Battle of Shiloh, but on the second day was fortunate to be ordered to escort prisoners back to Corinth.

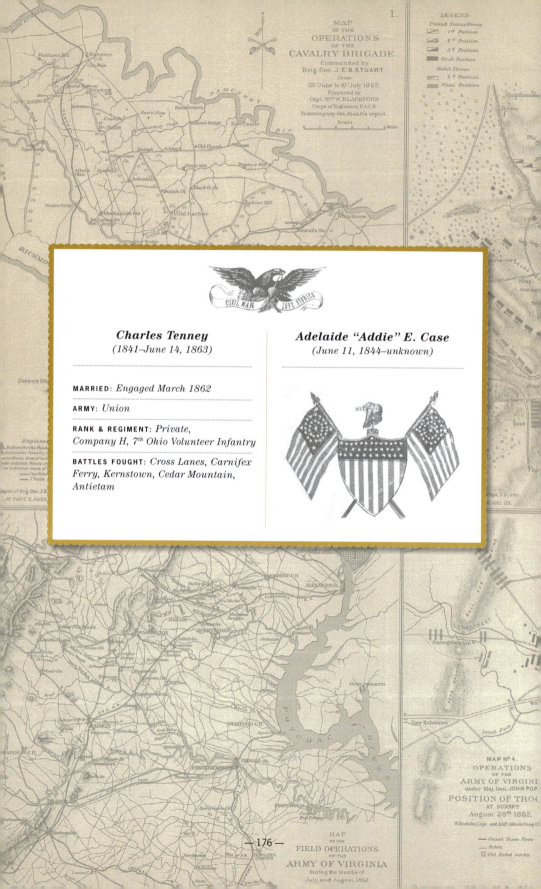

Charles Tenney
(1841–June 14, 1863)

Adelaide "Addie" E. Case
(June 11, 1844–unknown)

MARRIED: *Engaged March 1862*

ARMY: *Union*

RANK & REGIMENT: *Private,*
Company H, 7th Ohio Volunteer Infantry

BATTLES FOUGHT: *Cross Lanes, Carnifex*
Ferry, Kernstown, Cedar Mountain,
Antietam

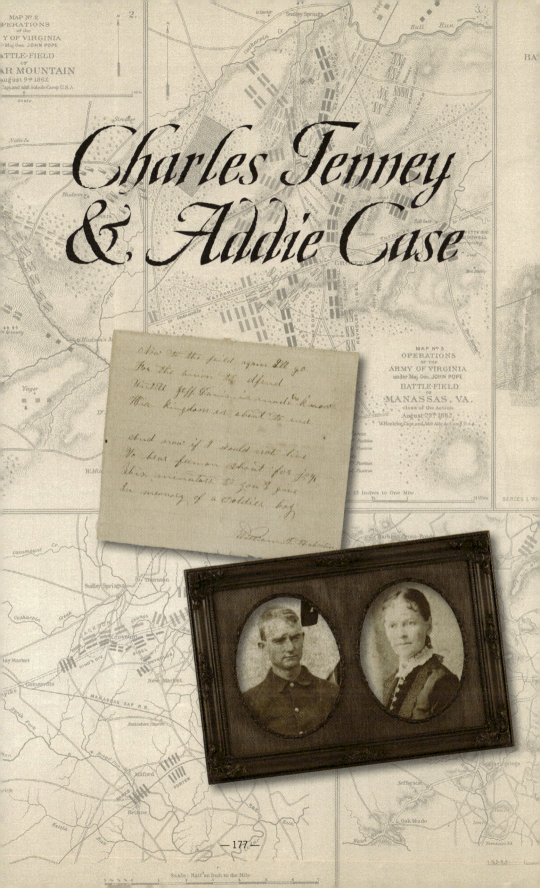

Charles Jenney
& Addie Case

Now to the field again I'll go
For the union I'll defend
Until Jeff Davis is made to know
His kingdom is about to end

And now if I should not live
To hear freemen shout for joy
This minuature to you I give
In memory of a Soldier boy

William M. Robertson

"*I dare not hope that you think more
of me than a common friend,*"

When the war began, Charles and Addie hadn't known each other for long, but she agreed to correspond with him after he told her he was estranged from his family and all alone in the world. His was a flirtatious correspondence that soon deepened into declarations of love, followed by a proposal of marriage.

Young men had different reasons for enlisting in the Union Army: some were patriotic to the Union and wanted to fight Secession; others hoped for a well-paid job and social advancement; a few believed they were following God's will—but Charles Tenney's motives were strictly personal. When war began in April 1861, his family was refusing to have anything to do with him on account of his dissolute lifestyle, but he hoped that distinguished conduct in the war might help him win his way back into his relatives' good graces. He had also met a young lady called Addie Case, whom he wanted to impress. He thought her beautiful, gentle, poetic, and musical, but feared she would never look at a man like him. He had no profession, and had acquired a reputation for drinking and gambling in their hometown of Mecca, Ohio. Perhaps if he enlisted to fight for the Unionist cause, she would view him in a more favorable light. It seemed worth a try.

Addie's brother Hal, a friend of his, was volunteering for the 7th Ohio, so Charles did the same. Before they left, he confided in Addie that he had no contact with his family, saying, "My home is not what a home should be," and asking if he might write to her. She was so touched that she agreed to correspond with him, but only "as a dear sister." Charles pushed for more, writing in his first letter, "I dare not hope that you think more of me than a common friend," and even asking her to send him her picture. She refused, telling him that only couples who were engaged should exchange

ABOVE
Addie took a lot of persuading before she would send Charles her picture.

OPPOSITE
Charles Tenney in camp, flanked by two comrades. Addie's letters were delightful; he said, "nothing could give me more pleasure—except a visit to the dear little author."

ABOVE
Camp Dennison often had as many as 12,000 inhabitants, and when it rained the fields became a sea of mud, but Charles described it as "pleasant" and urged Addie to visit.

pictures. Yet, at the same time, she told him she had "no kinder feelings" for friends she had known for many years than she now had for him. She liked him, but with reservations he would have to overcome before he could win her heart.

Nine long months of wooing

Charles and Hal trained at camps in Ohio and Cincinnati before being sent to western Virginia, where they saw their first action in September 1861 at Cross Lanes and then the Battle of Carnifex Ferry. "The day was won by our gallant Ohio boys," Charles wrote to Addie. "I cannot speak too highly of Hal." Hal had been promoted to lieutenant, and Charles often wrote of his great respect for him, knowing how much Addie loved her brother. "I really think of [him] as my own brother," he wrote, dropping a broad hint. But he also suffered an early bout of war weariness, writing in that same month that he'd be "glad when this cruel unholy war is ended. It seems so like killing friends."

Back in Ohio, Addie had a great fright when she opened a newspaper to see her brother wrongly listed as having been killed at Carnifex Ferry. It was later corrected, but she wrote that "Suspense is almost as bad as reality," and begged Charles to reassure her of his own safety.

Charles wrote often, and soon proved himself something of a poet, with memorable descriptions of the scenes his unit passed: "A gentle breeze murmurs by and ripples the clear and beautiful waters of the Kanawha," he wrote in one letter. In January 1862 he wrote her a poem about the "wondrous pow'r" of love. He also sent her an engraving of Camp Dennison, copied out extracts from his diary about camp life, and often drew little sketches to illustrate his letters.

Addie asked about the cause of the rift with his family, wondering in particular why his sister did not correspond with him. Charles was evasive: "I know of no reason unless she partakes of the prejudices which the entire family seem to hold against me." He didn't specify what these prejudices might be, but Addie's sister Laurie made a suggestion around Christmas 1861. "Laurie won't let me rest till I ask you if you got intoxicated," she wrote to him. He replied indignantly on January 1, 1862, "Did you wonder if [I] was engaged in some Bechanalian excesses?" He lied to her that he never was intoxicated in his life and, furthermore, had

GAMES OF CHANCE

Once a camp was established, soldiers often stayed there for months on end, with little to do except basic maintenance of weapons and horses, cooking meals, cleaning, and digging ditches. It was no wonder that they found all manner of entertainments to pass the time, including card games such as whist, cribbage, vingt-et-un (similar to blackjack), and quadrille. Dominoes, chess, and checkers were also popular, if someone should happen to have the pieces. For those without so much as a pack of cards, betting on lice or cockroach races could while away an idle hour or two. The competing insects were placed in the middle of a tin plate or sheet of canvas, and the first to cross the edge was the winner. Straight after payday, it wasn't uncommon for an entire month's wages to be lost at such events. Charles never admitted to gambling in any of his letters to Addie, but it seems unlikely that he never took part.

LEFT
Drinking whiskey and playing cards: some Union soldiers pass the time.

CAMP HOOCH

According to Union general McLellan, drunkenness was "the cause of by far the greater part of the disorders which are examined by court martials." Both armies banned enlisted men from purchasing alcohol, but the soldiers were adept at smuggling it into camp, and if they couldn't buy it they simply made their own. One Union recipe for hooch consisted of bark juice, tar water, turpentine, brown sugar, and alcohol. In the South, they sometimes dropped in some raw meat and let it ferment for a month or so. Names for camp hooch included "pop skull," "knock em stiff," and "oh be joyful." "We have lost more valuable lives at the hands of the whiskey sellers than by the balls of our enemies," said Confederate general Braxton Bragg.

RIGHT
Union general Ulysses S. Grant had a well-known fondness for whiskey.

pledged to become a teetotaller. He said he had "over two months ago eschewed the use of tobacco in any form," and had forsworn "the practice of playing cards." However, he added that the "temptations of a soldier's life were great," and hinted that it would be good for him to have "some restraining influence at home."

Whether or not it was true that he had indeed given up all "domestic evils," Addie seemed reassured, and later that month, after he had written a passionate love letter telling her that he loved her with "a pure, fervent affection that comes welling up from my heart," she replied in kind: "I will confess that I could love you with the true and fervent passion of which my heart is capable." At last she consented to send him a picture, and he was delighted, knowing that for her it represented a genuine commitment.

The 7th Ohio was in increasing danger as its men were sent out to stop the advance of General Robert E. Lee's Army of Northern Virginia, and perhaps this instilled in Charles a more urgent desire to put their relationship on a firm footing. On March 3, he was confident enough to try a clumsy proposal: "How would you like to change your name to the one I have?" he wrote on the third page of his letter, amidst other news from the company. She accepted his proposal, saying, "God in heaven help me to become worthy of such a noble heart," and calling him, "my precious one, my heart, my idol, my all."

Life on the home front

Addie was a great lover of music and enjoyed playing the melodeon (a kind of organ). She wrote to Charles in October 1861, saying that she had learned a new piece entitled "Mother dear O! pray for me." She also occupied her time during the first year of the war doing needlework with her "sweet little friend" Dora Leslie, and between them they sent Charles a gift of some needlepoint. By February 1862, she was making her own contribution to the war effort by volunteering for a Soldier's Aid Society, where she sewed bandages and other garments. In one corner, she said, sat the "Mecca Belles" (the pretty young girls from their hometown), in another the "young married people," while the older ladies were cooking chickens to be sent to the hospital for sick soldiers.

Also in February, she began work as a schoolteacher, in charge of "fifty scholars ranging in age from the blooming girl of twenty down to the lisping child of four years." At first just helping out, she was soon asked to take a six-month post in Claridon, Ohio, and she wrote to Charles, asking what she should do. His letters weren't getting through quickly enough, so she felt obliged to accept the offer, and straightaway took to the work. "Is not a school room the place to study human nature!" she wrote after her first day there on May 5, 1862, apparently very happy in her new post. Some of her scholars were "so far advanced" that she thought they might be able to teach her,

> "*How would you like to change your name to the one I have?*"

ABOVE
In 1861 and 1862, Charles wrote fifty-eight letters to Addie, and she wrote over seventy back to him.

rather than the other way around. She had thirty in her care, studying arithmetic, geography, grammar, algebra, and orthography, and she wrote to Charles about the textbooks she was using as well as the subjects they were covering.

Meanwhile, things were not going so well for her fiancé. He was wounded in the arm (though not seriously) at the Battle of Kernstown in March 1862, then lost dozens of his comrades in August at the Battle of Cedar Mountain. Of his company, 290 went into battle and only 104 came out. He only survived after being given the task of leading off the Colonel's wounded horse, which took him out of the line of fire. Worse was to come at the Battle of Antietam in September, however, from where he wrote that "the dead lay in heaps of tens, twenties, fifties, and even hundreds!"

Addie did not respond well to his letters describing danger. She was an anxious soul who worried constantly for Charles's safety. Every time she heard of a battle she feared that he might be in it. When he wrote, "My life is nothing, if by its sacrifice our country can be saved," she replied that if he died, she would wish to follow.

BELOW
The Battle of Antietam, September 17, 1862: General Burnside's troops had to cross a narrow stone bridge over a creek while Confederate sharpshooters picked them off from the wooded slopes nearby.

BATTLE OF ANTIETAM—TAKING OF THE BRIDGE ON ANTIETAM CREEK.

That summer Charles wrote to Addie's father officially asking for her hand in marriage, and on August 18 he received a somewhat equivocal reply: "If it is your and Addie's wish to connect your destinies for life, you shall have my best wishes and approval, unless that I shall learn of some dishonor attached to you, or her." Perhaps he already knew of Charles's reputation; his own family certainly hadn't forgiven him for past crimes. As he wrote to Addie in

ABOVE
Confederate dead lying in a row near Dunker Church after the Battle of Antietam.

October, even now that he was "defending the flag," they still gave him "a cold shoulder." He had written to them several times and received no reply.

When she heard this, Addie burst into tears, and wrote, "How could parents act so indifferently?" How indeed? It seems there may have been flaws in their son's character of which Addie was not aware—flaws that would soon cause him to become gravely ill.

Ill and far from home

In the second half of 1862, Charles's letters became less frequent, which drove Addie frantic with anxiety, leading her to profess her own feelings more ardently: "Surely man was never more worthy of my love than my noble, true-hearted Charlie." Perhaps she worried that he had found another girl, so it came as almost a relief when he wrote from Harper's Ferry, Virginia, on October 21 to tell her that he had been ill. He dismissed it as "that most horrible of all diseases 'Hypochondria'," and said he still felt a little "blue"—but in fact his illness was so serious that the doctor ordered him to stay behind and rest in hospital when his company moved on. Addie replied that his news had "troubled [her] a great deal," and she hoped he was entirely recovered.

On November 7, Charles wrote that he had been appointed a clerk in the Provost Marshal's office in Harper's Ferry, so he would be away from the fighting, which must have eased Addie's concerns. The illness recurred, though, and on the 17th he wrote, "I had a slight attack of Liver Complaint which troubled me some, but I am recovering from it now," adding that he was now "somewhat thinner and weaker" than when she had last seen him.

"Oh darling, how I wish you to come home," Addie wrote. "I would devote myself so much to your happiness that you could not fail to get well." On November 25, Charles wrote asking her what she would think of him if he were to accept a discharge from the army on medical grounds? Would she disapprove? She replied that although it might seem unpatriotic, she felt that he had already done his duty and should return as soon as possible. She was not to receive another letter from him.

> *"I can no longer conceal from thee dear, the suffering I have been compelled to endure since learning of your illness."*

Through December and January, Addie wrote regularly, bemoaning the length of time since she had heard from him. "I can no longer conceal from thee dear, the suffering I have been compelled to endure since learning of your illness." She prayed that God would make strangers care for him tenderly. In January she received word from friends in Charles's company that he had been given leave to come home but had suffered a relapse that meant he could not travel, and she wrote back asking them "to watch over Mr. Tenney as though he were as dear to you as he is to me."

There was no further word, and on April 13, 1863, Charles passed away in the hospital at Harper's Ferry. It seems likely that the cause of death was liver failure caused by the alcoholism he had always denied to Addie, but which his family was well aware of.

Charles's war service didn't win back the good opinion of his family, as he had hoped, and he would never walk down the aisle with his beloved Addie, but at least he died knowing that she believed him to be noble, true-hearted, and fully worthy of her love.

After the war, Addie married a man named George Benson Woodworth, with whom she had a daughter, but she would always keep the poetic letters and pretty sketches she had received from her wartime correspondent, friend, and lover, Charles.

HARPER'S FERRY

Sitting at the confluence of the Potomac and Shenandoah rivers, at the entrance to the Shenandoah Valley, the pretty town of Harper's Ferry was in such a strategically important position that it would change hands a total of eight times during the war years. Before that, in October 1859, abolitionist John Brown had attacked it, hoping to seize the weapons in the town's armory and incite African-American men to rise up against slavery. He failed, and was captured and executed. After the attack on Fort Sumter in April 1861, Union and Confederate troops alternated in taking the town. From February 1862, it was in Union hands until Stonewall Jackson took it at the Battle of Harper's Ferry on September 15, forcing the surrender of a large Union garrison. But he couldn't hold it, being obliged to hurry off to the Battle of Antietam, and a week later Charles Tenney's unit moved in. From then on, it was in Union hands except for eight days in July 1863 and a further four days in July 1864.

By the end of hostilities, the town had been ravaged by war: a visitor in 1866 wrote that "all about . . . are rubbish, and filth, and stench."

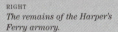

RIGHT
The remains of the Harper's Ferry armory.

BELOW
Harper's Ferry railroad bridge. Citizens rebuilt the town, only for most of their work to be undone by a flood in 1870.

Acknowledgments
Grateful thanks are due to the following for help with access to, and permission to quote from, Civil War letters:

Balou: Rhode Island Historical Society (special thanks to Katherine Chansky)

Black: Virginia Polytechnic Institute and State University Special Collections Department, "My Precious Loulie"

Demus: The Valley of the Shadow: Demus and Christie family letters, Virginia Center for Digital History, University of Virginia

Grier: Missouri History Museum Library and Research Center (special thanks to Molly Kodner)

Grow: www.longleaf.net/milo/ (special thanks to Gerald Grow)

Harrison: www.civilwarhome.com

Jackson: Virginia Military Institute

Love: The State Historical Society of Missouri (special thanks to Anne E. Cox)

Moxley: Center for American History at the University of Texas at Austin

Sheffey: John P. Sheffey Papers, Ms2001-060, Special Collections, Virginia Polytechnic Institute and State University, Blacksburg, VA.

Scott/Cone: www.civilwarletters.com (William Proudfoot)

Tenney/Case: The correspondence of Charles Tenney with Adelaide Case, Nettleton Collection, Special Collections Library, University of Virginia

Particular thanks to Jamie Pumfrey for help with research, to Jayne Ansell for being such an incredible editor, to Shelley Noronha for her ingenious picture research, to Wayne Blades and Andrew Milne for their stunning design, to Sophie Collins for making it happen, and to all the innovative team at Ivy Press.

And thanks to Karel Bata for watching Ken Burns's brilliant series *The American Civil War* with me (twice) and making useful suggestions about the text as I wrote it.

References
The following books were also very useful during my research:

Soldier of Southwestern Virginia: the Civil War letters of Captain John Preston Sheffey, edited by James I. Robertson, Jr., Louisiana State University Press, 2007

Rebels in Blue: The Story of Keith and Malinda Blalock, by Peter F. Stevens, Taylor Publishing Company, 2000

Beloved Bride: The Letters of Stonewall Jackson to his Wife, by William Potter, The Vision Forum Inc., 2002

The Civil War Letters of Dr. Harvey Black, edited by Glenn L. McMullen, Butternut and Blue, 1995

Oh, What a Loansome Time I Had, edited by Thomas W. Cutrer, The University of Alabama Press, 2002

The Heart of a Soldier, George E. Pickett, New York: Seth Moyle, c1913. (Available from University of Denver Penrose Library.)

Picture Credits:
Marilyn Ball: photo collection of, courtesy of Brad Blalock: *93L, 93R, 94L, 94R*

Black, Kent & Apperson Families: courtesy of Nita Black Little: 153R

Annalisa Bolin: courtesy of Robert G. & Ann Y. Avis: *141R, 142T*

Bridgeman Art Library: Atlanta Historical Society: *71, 127B, 128, 152T, 165;* Civil War Archive: *128;* Museum of the Confederacy, Richmond, VA: *154*

Ron Field: *18B, 20, 32, 44–45, 45R, 56–57, 57L, 57R, 62, 63, 68–69, 80, 92, 104–105, 116, 120, 128–129, 140-141, 152, 164–165, 176, 180, 184*

Gettysburg National Park: National Park Service, Museum Management Program and Gettysburg National Park: *181R, 105, 172, 182*

Gerald Grow: courtesy of great-grandson of Milo & Kate, www.longleaf.net.milo: *69R, 69L, 79*

Getty Images: *171*

Brenda Hoss: 102

Library of Congress: *6, 7, 8, 9, 10, 11T, 11B, 12, 13, 14, 15, 16L, 16R, 18, 19, 22, 25, 26, 27T, 28, 31, 33, 35, 37, 39, 40, 42, 43, 48, 49, 50, 51, 53, 54, 58T, 58B, 60, 61, 65, 66–67, 70T, 70B, 71, 72, 73, 74, 76T, 76B, 78–79, 83, 84, 85T, 85C, 85B, 86, 87, 88, 91, 97, 98, 99T, 99B, 101, 103T, 103B, 105, 106, 107, 108–109, 109, 111, 112, 113, 114, 117L, 119, 120, 121, 123, 124, 125, 127T, 127C, 129L, 134–135, 135, 137, 138, 139, 144–145, 145, 146, 149, 150, 156, 158, 160, 162, 166, 169T, 169B, 170, 173, 174–175, 177T, 181, 184, 185, 187T, 187B*

Marshall University: Special Collections, Huntington, West VA: *23, 24, 29, 129R, 137*

Missouri History Museum: *33R, 34, 36, 141L, 142, 147, 151;* Arthur Love, Australia: *33L*

National Archives & Records Administration: Washington D.C. Record Group 15, Records of the Bureau of Veterans Affairs, Case File of Wesley Krunkleton, Alias David Demus: *57*

National Park Service: Museum Management Program and Gettysburg National Park: GETTY31374 song book: *81R;* GETT42096 prayer book: *105R;* GETT8241 tin of quinine: *172;* GETT31373 bottle of Bourbon: *182*

Ohio Historical Society: 55

Bill Proudfoot: *81C, 81L*

Rhode Island Historical Society: courtesy of J.A. O'Niell: Sullivan Ballou, Rhode Island c.1860. ink on paper, RHiX36402: *117, 118;* letter to his wife, Sarah (transcription), Washington D.C., July 14, 1861, ink on paper, RHiX36440-6441: *121*

State Library of North Carolina: Hugh Morton: *96;* Southern Historical Collection: *92*

Ken Thomas: *95*

Topfoto: *38;* The Granger Collection: *17T, 17B, 27B, 136, 155, 157*

University of North Carolina at Chapel Hill: *92–93, 96*

University of Texas at Austin: Moxley (William M.) Papers, the Dolph Briscoe Center for American History: *165*

University of Virginia: Albert and Shirley Small Special Collections Library, Charles Tenney & Adelaide Case: *177BL, 177BR, 178, 179;* MSS 11616, Letters of Charles Tenney, Camp Kelly, VA.,1861-1863: *178, 183*

Virginia Military Institute Archives: courtesy of: *21L, 21R, 24–25, 30*

Virginia Polytechnic Institute & State University: University Libraries, Special Collections, George Doyle Scrapbook (Ms1989-096): *32, 56, 80, 104, 176;* John P. Sheffey Papers (Ms2001-060): *46;* Black, Kent and Apperson Families (Ms1974-003): *153;* Collection of United Daughters of the Confederacy: *161*

Whatcom Museum of History of Art: Bellingham, WA: 1994004600000: *130;* X2879000001: *132*

Images p45, courtesy of the descendents of Preston and Josie Sheffey/James I Robinson

QUOTATIONS

In most instances, original spellings and grammar have been used in quotations from the letters, although punctuation has sometimes been added for clarity.

MONEY EQUIVALENTS

To give a rough idea of prices mentioned in the book, a dollar in 1865 would be worth $14.08 today. Eggs cost 20 cents a dozen, bread was 2 cents a loaf, land sold for $3 to $5 an acre, and a laborer's wage without board was 90 cents a day. However, prices in the South varied widely throughout the war as inflation destroyed the economy.